GET YOUR BUTT OFF MY COUCH
(AND YOUR HAND OUTTA MY WALLET)

Sonja Warfield

Thank you for your purchase.

Great reviews mean everything to a writer. If you enjoyed this book in any way, please take a moment to let me, and other readers, know what you thought. Once again, thank you and enjoy!

GET YOUR BUTT OFF MY COUCH
(AND YOUR HAND OUTTA MY WALLET)
©2015 by Sonja Warfield
Limited Print/ebook Edition

All rights reserved. Without limiting the rights under copyright reserved above, no parts of this publication may be reproduced, stored in or introduced into a retrieval system, or transmitted, in any form, or by any means (electronic, mechanical, photocopying, recording, or otherwise) without the prior written permission of the copyright owner of this book. Some parts of this work are fiction. Names, characters, places, brands, media, and incidents are either the product of the author's imagination or are used fictitiously.

Edition License Notes

This book is licensed for your personal enjoyment only. This e-book may not be re-sold or given away to other people. If you would like to share this book with another person, please purchase a copy for each person you share it with. If you are reading this book and did not purchase it, or it was not purchased for your use only, then please purchase your own copy. Thank you for respecting the author's work.

ACKNOWLEDGEMENTS

I'd like to acknowledge God, not that He needs my acknowledgment because He is... God, after all. I'm so grateful for everything God has given me. I appreciate the hills and valleys of this life and the lessons I'm learning as I go. I am so blessed and grateful to be able to share these stories with you. In this book I offer my stories and stories shared with me by friends and acquaintances I've met through the years.

So many people inspired me to write this book. I want to name several. Without their support, laughs, stories, encouragement, prayers, time and love, the book would not exist. Thank you Norman, Mom, Dad, Cheryl, Paula, Stephanie, Aunt Barbara, Jenny, Kelli, Jill, Tricia, Camille, Rhonda, Krista, Wendy, Demetrius, Shirley, Mireya, Maya, Carole, Nancy, Eric, Nadia, Kim, Chris, Quinn, Malcolm Lee, Janet Hill and everyone else who inspired and helped me. Burnie Dyment, I am indebted and grateful for your help, friendship and love. Thank you to Kim Collier. I seriously could not have done this without you, girl. Thank you to everyone who laughed out loud when I told you the title of this book. And thank you, Lord, for somehow enabling me to finish. My hope and prayer is that my stories will inspire and bless your life in some way.

I dedicate this book to my favorite son, Mr. Norman.

"Do not go where the path may lead, go instead where there is no path and leave a trail."

Ralph Waldo Emerson

DEDICATION

I dedicate this book to every woman...
   ... who has ever worn two pairs of Spanx under her jeans to make her ass more appealing to some guy.
   ...who has ever tried to make an eloquent point with lipstick on her teeth.
   ...who has worn six-inch heels that aren't a job requirement, like if you were a hooker or a talk show host or an aspiring Kardashian.
   ...who have gotten their good Indian hair extensions caught in a headboard.
   ... who has fake laughed so hard at some loser guy's jokes that you peed a little.
   ... who has been forced to watch other people kiss on New Year's Eve, or spent a sad, lonely, acid-reflux Valentine's Day alone watching *The Real Housewives of New Jersey* marathon, which just makes you realize that you'll probably never be a real housewife of anything, not even a double wide in El Paso.
   ...who has ever loved her wedding dress more than she

loved her husband.

...who has ever imagined her husband or boyfriend dying in a plane crash as an easier method to ending the relationship than just telling him you aren't in love anymore and the sight of his face makes you puke up your breakfast.

...who has ever thrown herself on her bed á la Scarlett O'Hara over a break-up, divorce, non-call or ambiguous text message from some guy who you don't even like that much, but was your best shot at having a New Year's Eve kiss or half-ass Valentine's Day date. I feel you, girl. We've all been there.

...who has cried over love and/or lusted after Channing Tatum, Usher, Michael B. Jordan, or Rob Lowe from the 80's especially in that shower scene in *The Outsiders* or the shower scene in *About Last Night*. Basically anything where he's half-naked and wet. He's not bad in those Direct TV ads either.

I also dedicate this book to all the men who have loved the women described above. (I apologize to my 6th grade teacher, Mrs. Esselstyn for ending my previous sentence in a preposition.)

I'd like to thank my editor, my girlfriends and every loser who has ever taken up space on some woman's couch.

Good reading and good luck.

TABLE OF CONTENTS

ACKNOWLEDGEMENTS iii

DEDICATION v

INTRODUCTION ix

CHAPTER ONE: Boys Will Be Boys Is Bullshit 3

CHAPTER TWO: Don't Get A 'D' In Dating 19

CHAPTER THREE: Dick Is Not An Endangered Species ... 43

CHAPTER FOUR: They Shoot 40-Year Old Women Don't They? 59

CHAPTER FIVE: You Can Change Him Girl, Is a Lie 69

CHAPTER SIX: Our Bodies and the Bodies We Covet 85

CHAPTER SEVEN: Post Traumatic Dating Disorder Recovery Plan 113

CHAPTER EIGHT: Men and Irritable Bowel Syndrome ... 125

CHAPTER NINE: Men Who Go Missing 139

CHAPTER TEN: Breaking Up Is Hard To Do, But Getting Dumped Can Suck It!........155

CHAPTER ELEVEN: Tennis, Love and the Truth.............165

CHAPTER TWELVE: Desperation in Life and Love........181

CHAPTER THIRTEEN: Fear, Faith & Being Single.........189

CHAPTER FOURTEEN: Afraid to Hope............................223

CHAPTER FIFTEEN: Feelings Whoa, Whoa, Whoa Feelings... 237

CHAPTER SIXTEEN: So Long Farewell and Adieu To Fear........241

CHAPTER SEVENTEEN: Almost Divorced......................249

CHAPTER EIGHTEEN: Fight On!......................277

ABOUT THE AUTHOR..................281

INTRODUCTION

This book is a guide to getting rid of your deadbeat husband, boyfriend, or your boo thing. A boo thing is the guy who occasionally calls you late at night, or just shows up at your doorstep and might even take you out to eat–but never to anything fancier than 2 for 1 night at Applebee's. You know what I'm talking about. We've all been there. You're lonely, vulnerable and rather than spending another sad, single Saturday night watching Bridget Jones' romantic calamities again, you respond to the late night text. In fact, your boo thing may be sitting next to you right now. Well, keep reading girl because this book will help you get his ass off of your couch.

Another edition of this book is titled: Big Fat Negro, Get Your Lazy Ass Off My Couch. Now the term Negro may offend or surprise people. I'm not trying to bring Negro back like Justin Timberlake brought sexy back. I'm just trying to bring it out of hiding for a minute. My use of the word describes men from my life and my girlfriends' lives who took up residence on our collective couches. Some of those men just happened to be black. I didn't feel as if lazy and fat were disparaging enough to describe the quality of their character, so I reached back into the fabric of American history--racism, and co-opted a word that at one time did not have such a negative connotation. That being said any woman can insert her man's ethnic persuasion into this title. For example: "Big, Dumb, Drunk, Redneck Get Your Lazy Ass Out of My Doublewide." I added 'drunk' here because in my mind, I pictured an intoxicated, white trash jerk who is on the couch perpetually watching *Duck Dynasty* and engaging in some sort of flatulence contest with himself and Honey Boo Boo on television. Or, if he's of Latin origin: "Gordo Machismo Latino, Perdedor, Quita Tu Pinche Culo Huevon de Mi Sillion." Or, "Stupid, Italian, Stallion Get Your Lazy, Greasy, Fat, Tony Soprano Ass Off My Couch." Or, "Overprivileged, Cold-Blue-Blooded Wasp, Get Your Thin Lipped, Entitled, Flat Ass Off My Eames Lounge Chair." Or, " Lazy, Grown Ass Pothead, Get Your X-Box Playing, Skateboard Riding Ass Off My Futon." There's probably some lazy ass Gypsy husband or boyfriend out there who isn't pulling his weight in cons. And if any of those names are offensive, or don't fit the bill then: Get Your Butt Off My Couch And Your Hand Outta My Wallet will work for you. Essentially, deadbeat husbands and boyfriends transcend ethnicity and religion and they don't have to be big and fat. In this book, you'll read about my relationship stories and my girlfriends' relationship stories. All the names have been changed to protect the losers on the couch and the ones who loved them.

The civil rights activist Fannie Lou Hamer's famous quote serves as my inspiration for writing this book. She said in reference to the civil rights struggle: "I am sick and tired of being sick and tired." Well, I am sick and tired of hearing stories about triflin' men and the women who put up with their shit. If you think you have a loser on your couch, understand that you are culpable. You have given him an invitation to sit on your couch and hold you back from living life to the fullest.

If you're reading this book, you are too smart and too fantastic to be wasting your time with a loser, so be loosed of him and get on with your life, girl! We're all sisters in the adventures of dating and marriage and we have to look out for one another. We need to love ourselves enough to take back our couches and our lives. The intention of this book is not to blame, nor bash men. We enter into relationships as a couple and screw them up together. I just happen to be a woman so I'm writing about my experiences and friends' experiences in relationships with men that didn't work out from the female prospective. Many of the same criticisms I put forth about men can also be attributed to women, but that's a whole other book. I believe in marriage, hope, reconciliation, forgiveness and love. So grab a bottle of wine and some girlfriends as you read Part One. Swap stories, laughs and lessons in love.

In Part Two the party is winding down. It's time to get real. So you may want to put the coffee on and pour a cup. What I've learned about dating and relationships really applies to all aspects of life. So I had to dig deep and figure out who I am and why I allowed a man to take up residence on my couch in the first place. In Part Two you'll read about my life excavation; the relics of pain that I dug up and set free to get to the most important love of my life: me.

What qualifies me to write such book you may I ask? First of all, I'm a licensed comedy writer. I've been married and divorced. I paid alimony. I've been dating for thirty years except for the years I was married and I've been in therapy for more than twenty years. I'm daring enough to say something like: Get Your Butt Off My Couch And Your Hand Outta My Wallet, so who knows what else I'm going to say inside this book.

Good Morning America's Robin Roberts says, "Make your mess your message." That's exactly what I've done with this book.

PART ONE

CHAPTER ONE

Boys Will Be Boys Is Bullshit

"**B**oys will be boys" is bullshit. Because it is... bullshit. There are a whole host of offenses and behavior that women excuse by saying, "Boys will be boys." When we say "Boys will be boys" we do not expect or demand them to act like responsible, adult men so we get boys. You know those parents you see in the store who try to reason or negotiate with their screaming, belligerent, spoiled kids. Those are the parents who would rather be friends with their kids and shy away from discipline, so their children don't learn how to comport themselves. Their children only repeat the bad behavior and so will a grown man unless a woman will call him on his bullshit. An Undisciplined Child grows up to become an entitled adult who doesn't understand why the world doesn't bend to his will and continues misbehaving and treating people without respect because he had no home training. He becomes a grown ass, triflin' man who ends up arriving at a party with one date, but leaving with some other woman, forcing date number one to Uber it home. He becomes a man who stops paying child support because his new girlfriend thinks that money can be put to better use on a romantic getaway instead of the costly braces to fix his kid's teeth. He becomes the loser who is sitting on your couch, taking up space and not contributing to anyone's greater good. Ladies, we need to stop saying, "Boys will be boys."

We also need to stop saying: "Guys do stupid things." If your guy does something stupid, then guess what: he is stupid. Do you want to forever be linked with stupidity? When we make these excuses for men it's as if we're saying: whatever reprehensible behavior he did is excused because he has a penis. Now I've never heard anyone excuse a woman's bad behavior in a relationship by saying, "Girls will be girls" therefore she deserves a pass, but women do it every day for men. You've probably said it to your friends, your sister, your divorced mother who is desperately trying to interpret her new handsome co-worker's lukewarm advances and inability to call her back. Some women have arsenals full of excuses for men. Why do you think women marry death row inmates? Yes, crazy has something to do with it, but there are excuses and lies women tell themselves wrapped up in the crazy package.

Let me tell you about my friend and her triflin' husband, but in this instance my friend chose to stop making excuses when she had a pivotal "Boys will be boys is bullshit" moment.

How Kate Knew Her Marriage Was Over...Thanks Oprah

My dear friend Kate was married for six years. Most people can't point to a single incident or crystallizing moment when they knew their marriage was over, but Kate can. It was the day she came home from a long hard day at work to find her husband on the couch. He was unemployed at the time, so he had been home all day. Their nanny had left. Their baby was asleep. There was no dinner waiting for her, no kiss hello, but there hadn't been any of those things in a long time. The only thing she was looking forward to that night, short of seeing her sleeping child, was watching *Oprah*. At that point in her marriage, Oprah was the one who gave her joy. Now this was over a decade ago when Oprah's show was still on the air. Also, this was the beginning of DVR technology and they had not yet invested in a TIVO, but she still had her VCR and every day it was set at three o'clock to tape her *Oprah*. So that night, she passed by her husband, they exchanged a few terse, declarative sentences and she retreated into the bedroom, got in bed, turned on the TV, hit play on the VCR and got ready for *Oprah*, but to her dismay *Oprah* did not appear on screen. Instead a naked man and women who seemed to be engaging in a threesome-orgy appeared. She tried to decipher the nasty, naked body parts. *That's not Oprah.* Trying to process the images, she tilted her head to the side befuddled and perplexed. *Now that sure isn't Oprah.* Where the hell was her *Oprah*? If her Godforsaken husband interfered with her Oprah recording that was a deal breaker in the marriage.

    She took the tape out of the VCR. It had one of those alliterate porn titles and pictures of shiny, fake boobs. She confronted her husband with the evidence. There would be no: "Boys will be boys" excuse for this bullshit. He didn't deny that he was watching the porn tape. When she asked him what happened to her *Oprah*, he said he must have shut off the VCR when it was supposed to record. There were no words. She wasn't as upset about the demise of her marriage or the porn. The real offense was screwing with her *Oprah*. It was egregious and quite frankly unforgivable. Had he been able to produce a tape of that day's episode of *Oprah* and if they had even watched it as a couple maybe *Oprah* could have been the glue that bonded them back together, but instead the moment was as Oprah would say her "ah-ha moment" when she knew her marriage was over.

    Kate could have excused her husband's porn watching and disregard for *Oprah* by saying: "Boys will be boys" and she'd probably still be in that loveless marriage today, but Kate said no more excuses and she called him on his shit and stopped enabling him by allowing bad behavior and excusing it with cliched sayings.

Yet Another Triflin' Story

I have a friend who was renting a house that was owned by a married couple. The husband, her landlord, started to become friendly with my friend, his tenant. He started texting her at all hours, especially late at night. Now I don't know about you, but I've never received texts from any landlord late at night unless it involved a plumbing emergency. Eventually he made sexual advances. She told him she wasn't interested, reminded him that he was married, but he kept at it. He texted her a photo of-- yes, his genitals. My friend couldn't understand how this man, an intelligent, married, <u>attorney</u> would do something so stupid as to text a picture of his genitals to his tenant. Clearly he was suffering from Anthony Weiner syndrome. The most shameful thing about the entire incident was that he didn't even bother to photoshop his dick pic and make himself more of a man than he'd ever be. Of course my friend shared the pictures with her other girlfriends (P.S. to all you would-be penis selfie taking dudes, we share those photos and we evaluate your male parts over wine and snarky laughter). We all agreed this landlord motherfella was suffering from P.I.S., Penis Illusion Syndrome, a disorder that causes men to think their genitalia is bigger, better and even bionic when the reality is that it's less than mediocre.

My friend called her girlfriends together to brainstorm a

means to stop her landlord from being a nasty bastard. Some of the women shook their heads in disbelief at his offenses. Others weren't surprised because "Guys do stupid things" and "Boys will be boys." Although Judge Judy's name was bandied about, we couldn't really come up with any legal recourse for my friend against her landlord that wouldn't cost her in humiliation, time and dollars. Others thought she should text the photos to his wife. My favorite idea was to post printouts of the photos all around the neighborhood similar to what people do when they post pictures of lost dogs, but instead of writing: "lost dog" she'd write: "In search of pitiful penis owner." My friend chose to move instead of retaliate. Her lascivious landlord sexually harassed her out of her house and he's probably still doing that to other women. But that shouldn't be surprising because we live in a patriarchal, boys will be boys, Anthony Weiner world.

It is true guys do stupid things. It's not an excuse, but it is a reality. All the blood rushes out of their head and down to the other one. Stupidity ensues. Again the stupidity is inexcusable, but it is a fact. As women we need to hold them to a higher standard.

They Check In, But They Don't Check Out

Boys who misbehave and then get a slap on the wrists for their misbehavior do it again and again until someone like

GET YOUR BUTT OFF MY COUCH

Carrie Underwood in her song "Before He Cheats" gets up enough nerve to "slash a hole in all four tires" before his dumb ass cheats on her again. I like Carrie Underwood. I voted for her on *American Idol*, but the problem with your song, Carrie, is that you think you're helping women, but you're not. All your wisdom about "slashing a hole in all four tires and carving your name into his leather seats," is vandalism and it just makes the woman who does that look like a crazy, psycho b-i-t-c-h. Not as crazy as the chick from *Gone Girl*, but neither image helps the feminist cause. Plus the jerk from Carrie Underwood's song who cheated can just go to Costco, buy three tires and get the fourth one free, and have them installed while he's eating lunch. So it's not much of a deterrent. I understand why Carrie sings about this and I understand the woman who vandalizes the car. This woman is suffering from P.T.D.D., Post Traumatic Dating Disorder. And I have my own ideas about remedies for this condition.

The 1987 film *Fatal Attraction* exposed the less glamorous side of cheating. I've got to give it to Glenn Close, her performance left men terrorized, but that was almost thirty years ago. A new disincentive to cheating is needed. And I've created one. It's called B.D.S., Broken Dick Syndrome. My dad used to tell me that a guy will stick "it" anywhere. And by "it" he was referring to the penis. The best deterrent, if they will in fact stick it anywhere, is that when they stick it someplace it's

NOT supposed to be, they won't get it back. There used to be a commercial slogan for The Roach Motel that said, "Roaches check in, but they don't check out." In my myth, the errant penis would suffer the same fate as the roaches.

Here is how the urban legend will go. A husband and father of three is asked by his wife to go to the store and get some milk. While wandering through the grocery store, he notices a woman in the potato chip aisle. He checks the woman out and decides he'd rather snack on her than a bag of Doritos. She seems game. He follows her into the grocery store restroom. They don't exchange names or salutations this is nasty, dirty, midnight grocery store, bathroom sex. When they're finished, he finds that he cannot remove his penis from her. It's stuck. He has just had sex with the roach motel of vaginas. After an intense struggle, pain, writhing and gnashing of teeth, he's able to remove what's left of his member from her vaginal abyss, but it's literally broken, withered, and considerably smaller than it ever was. The life, girth and erectile abilities have been sucked out of his penis. He returns home a broken man. The first thing his wife asks him is where the hell is the milk. If he had done as he was told, he'd have a dick, a wife, kids and a gallon of milk. Now he has nothing, not even his manhood. He seeks medical attention, but doctors tell him this is a rare vascular disease for which there is no cure: Broken Dick Syndrome. Because the blood flow has been permanently altered soon his dick will just shrivel up and fall off. This story will become an urban legend, it will spread across the internet like the viral video of the adult lions meeting their trainers after years of separation, but this would scare men worse than *Fatal Attraction*. It may seem like a highly unlikely story. Men may not believe it, but it may raise a tiny sliver of doubt that will cause them to think before they cheat, at least more than that Carrie Underwood song--no offense, Carrie.

A Blow Job Strike

In thinking about what we as women can do in terms of consequences for boyfriends, husbands and dates who behave badly, I've come up with the ultimate consequence. When my son was younger and he'd misbehave, I took away his favorite toy. It was usually a Batman type of toy, which was like taking away a limb. As kids get older, parents usually take away their phones, to punish them, which are basically their lifelines.

In dating we have to give these men some consequences for their bad behavior. I have an idea of a major consequence that could be the biggest deterrent to male bad behavior: a blowjob strike.

My grandfather worked for Republic Steel and strikes were a part of life because the workers were not getting fair pay and treatment, so their boss had to be taught a lesson in the form of a work stoppage. The only ammunition the Republic Steel workers had against the corporation was themselves and their work. They were not being valued for their contribution to the corporation, so they stopped showing up for work and the boss started to pay attention. After absorbing the loss of a complete work stoppage, the corporation would become amenable to meeting with union leaders and negotiating with their workers to give them what they wanted and needed and stop their unfair business practices that were detrimental to the work force.

In the term blowjob, work is obvious. The blowjob work stoppage I'm proposing has to be organized. We have to have a platform, meetings, support systems and our message to the men has to be clear. Albeit, the message will differ for each woman, but it has to be cohesive in order to get our power back. We need buttons and picket lines and group hugs. I say we strike for a month (and not one of those short months like February given to Black history, but a long one like March or July). We need to make this an international strike because men will be crossing all sorts of borders to get some head. Canada will see a bigger influx of American men than they did during the draft dodging years.

It may sound extreme, but if we collectively as women find ourselves in untenable relationships with men who are not treating us right, a blowjob strike is a nice idea to ponder and toss out there on the Internet (to go viral) as a real possibility.

It may just scare your man enough to get him to act right.

Married women can and should strike too. We can't "bring home the bacon, fry it up in a pan" as the Enjoli ad from the 80's said, and take care of the kids. It's too much. Something's got to give. When women feel overwhelmed, blowjobs are usually the first thing to go anyway. Let's be honest ladies, most of us will be less likely to go downtown if we've been working all day, your man's ass has been on a couch all day and when we come home there's no dinner, the kids have not been bathed, laundry hasn't been done and bills have not been paid.

Fair Treatment In Relationships

There needs to be an equitable, gender neutral distribution of household chores and child care. Yes, I know men can't breastfeed, but they can cook. Here's the thing if you are the female and the breadwinner in your marriage and your nanny is sick, the entire childcare issue should not suddenly fall directly on your shoulders. That is a situation my friend Mallory found herself in when her nanny called in sick and her part-time working husband told the nanny to call his wife and tell her she couldn't report to work because he was busy; therefore, full-time working Mallory had to find alternate child care while she was busy working at the job that made her the breadwinner. Ladies *that* may be an issue you have to strike over. Had Mallory's husband been denied blowjobs for three months after said behavior, he'd probably have that nanny's number on speed dial, as well as back-up child care and on his days off he'd be taking care of the child, cooking and doing laundry.

I felt empowered and moved by Patricia Arquette's 2015 Academy Award acceptance speech in which she gave voice to a woman's right to equal pay. I stand together with her. We also need to stand up for another cause: fair treatment in dating and relationships. Really the onus of expecting better behavior from men in relationships is on women. There is no excuse for bad behavior. There is room for forgiveness in life. People are not perfect. The bad behavior I'm referring to is habitual and part of one's character as opposed to an act for which a man is truly repentant. The bottom line is, ladies, when a man doesn't call you back after sex, don't make up an excuse for him. When your man doesn't prioritize you, don't say he's too busy. As my dad used to tell me: "unless he's the President of the United States, he can call you back." When your man doesn't come home all night, don't accept his lame excuse. When a man stands you up, don't think that he's had car trouble or an accident. I have a girlfriend who had a blind date with a man. En route to the date the man actually did get into a car accident, but he still showed up to the date only a few minutes late, but with a severely dented car. That is a man of his word.

Boys will be boys allows men to do what they want and get away with it from an early age so that the rules of society don't seem to apply to them. Think about it. There are more men in prison because they think they are above the law. Male teenage drivers cost more to insure than female drivers because insurance companies have data compiled that statistically shows young males break more traffic laws. Our society isn't asking teenage males to be better or more careful drivers. Their bad boy driving is expected, accepted and just costs a little more. In childhood, as women we're told to be "good girls," which means we have to follow rules and do as we're told and essentially people please. In the television series *The Good Wife*, Julianna Marguiles' character stopped taking her philandering husband's shit and created her own path and life for herself and her children. Good girls and good wives have the connotation of being complacent or silent partners who do as we're told. Society has branded us. Let's re-brand ourselves, ladies! Let's make our own rules. Let's stop being good girls and start doing what we want and getting what we ask for in everything.

We need to apply the same principle to lousy boyfriends and husbands as we do to terrorism. If you see something, say something. To combat this "Boys will be boys bullshit" we need to start a grass roots movement. It worked for Obama twice. We should use social media to energize and organize our base so that we as women stand together and say no more to these guys and their crap. President Obama signed the Lilly Ledbetter act into law for equal pay for women. Does he need to sign a new law for equality in dating to combat poor treatment and input new higher standards so that we don't settle for mediocrity or worse?

Top Ten Ways Your Behavior Changes in a Bad Relationship

1. He tells you where he's supposed to be and you do a "drive by" to make sure he's where he said he would be, but you don't want him to see you. So you duck down low in your car as you drive by. You're so low that only your hands can be seen on the steering wheel and you can't see the road so you hit a lamp post and lie about the accident.
2. You start embellishing his résumé to your friends, family and yourself.
3. You bought your own engagement ring, but you're pretending like he bought it.
4. You make rationalizations for his bad behavior e.g.: drinking, philandering, gambling, abuse and neglect.
5. You allow him to convince you to have sex without a

condom and without getting him checked for HIV first. When you go try on shoes at the mall, the sales people make you put on a ped to protect your feet. What's more important? Your feet, or your hoo-ha?
6. You've started planning and rationalizing your extramarital affair.
7. You have started swearing and yelling at him and you're not a yeller or someone who swears.
8. You make up excuses so you won't have to bring him to a party, or you leave the party early because he's embarrassing you.
9. You borrowed money out of your 401k to bail him out of jail more than once, but again kept it a secret.
10. He's been getting texts from a woman and one night you finally lose it and go Elin Woods on his ass with a baseball bat because your man doesn't play golf.

When you lie to yourself every day to try to convince yourself that your quasi, pathetic relationship is better than being alone, when you aren't acting like yourself anymore and you can't tell your friends and family the truth about your relationship something is wrong. When you're excusing his behavior and your behavior changes so much that you don't even recognize or like yourself anymore, it is time to move on.

CHAPTER TWO
Don't Get A 'D' In Dating

If a guy approaches you with his 'D' game and you accept that game, he's never going to try to do anything to raise his grade when he can get you to sleep with him, make him dinner and identify yourself as his woman by just giving you a 'D' effort. If you have a child and they come home with a 'D' on their report card and they do not have a learning disability, as a parent it's your job to make sure that child puts forth the effort to raise that grade. Don't settle for D's in life, unless it's your bra size and you're happy with it and it doesn't cause you back pain.

Power 106

After my divorce I was set-up on a series of blind dates. I refer to this time as my old, divorced, bachelorette days, sans Chris Harrison, the fantasy suite and the rose ceremony.

Sometimes there was a drunk, crying girl. And usually that was me. Anyway during this period, people felt sorry for me because I was divorced and alone and they felt like the best remedy for that was a man a.k.a.: new dick. For most of them, they didn't seem to put much into the thought of the set-ups, except that the man I was being set-up with was single too, in one case also divorced, two of them were writers, one an actor and another a producer and in most cases the bachelors were black. Black was the primary criteria for several matchmakers though that wasn't the case for me, but I wasn't asked. Unlike the real Bachelorette, there wasn't a casting agent doing the picking so my potential bachelors resembled the half price bin at Ross: odd shapes, sizes, varying amounts of hair, really short, tall and ill-mannered, and even one who I'm convinced was gay. I really don't know where they found these dudes: a halfway house; left swipe loser Tinder rejects. I actually wondered if some of my friends secretly hated me. Since I was newly divorced, alone and was made to feel like I needed to date because dating was the cure-all, I accepted these fix-ups, which really felt more like pity dating assignments. Really I don't think many of my friends would have taken no for an answer. So I had a series of first dates and all of them only amounted to first dates because this post divorce dating school is where I refined my standards and constructed many of my no bullshit policies for potential suitors. After going through a divorce, I was not about to waste another minute of my life with someone who was not lifting me up.

One of the set-ups was so exquisitely awful that at one point I actually thought I was being televised for one of those candid camera shows or *What Would You Do* on ABC News. Seriously, I was waiting for John Quinones from ABC to pop up from behind a potted plant and say we got you, Sonja. *This is not an actual date.* It was so terrible that in my mind it had to be a televised prank because this date was a domino car crash that just kept getting more horrifically unbelievable by the minute. In the annals of my dating history this date is always referred to as POWER 106.

In Hollywood writers have agents and sometimes managers. I had both. My manager at the time met with a prospective writer client, who happened to be a black man. The man, let's call him Jeff because I made a conscious choice to forget his name after the interminable 54 minute door-to-door quasi date I had with him. So my manager called me after meeting Jeff because he thought we'd make a great couple since we're both black and we're both writers. Yes, with that minimal criteria he thought we could build a life long, 'til death do us part union together. Anyway, I agreed to the date because again I felt pressure to accept dates as a remedy to being single, which I now know is not a terminal disease, but back then I wasn't convinced. So the guy, Jeff, calls me. We exchanged witty banter on the phone. We agreed to go out on a Friday night because my son would be with his father. Jeff called me Wednesday to see if I happened to be available to go out the next evening because he had movie premiere tickets to *Mission Impossible 3*.

    Living in Los Angeles and going to a movie premiere is sort of like a work/social event, but still fun and exciting. I've gone to my share of movie premieres. I've walked the red carpet, watched the movie and later attended the premiere after party. I was able to arrange things so I could go to the premiere. And then I did what any single girl prepping for a first date that had now been elevated to a first date at a red carpet event would do: I polled my girlfriends on what I should wear and then I made a crucial hair appointment. My date, Jeff, told me that he'd get back to me about what time he'd pick me up for the premiere on Thursday. I was at the salon most of the day because I am a black woman and getting your "hair did" is usually an all-day affair. (Not so much because it takes that long to do your hair, but my stylist had attitude, drama and wall-to-wall clients.) I became a little concerned when I didn't hear from Jeff early in the day, but he finally called in the afternoon to tell me he'd pick me up at 4pm. Most premieres begin after 7pm so I thought 4pm was odd, but this was *Mission Impossible 3* and Tom Cruise and Katie Holmes had just had baby Suri, plus they're Scientologists, so I thought okay maybe they do things differently and there's some sort of movie premiere Scientology Sabbath ritual.

    Jeff picked me up. This was before I was on Facebook so it was literally a blind date. He wasn't bad looking, but I wasn't immediately attracted either. What I did notice about him that was odd were his green-colored contact lenses. And it was more than odd. To me it's weird and off-putting for a regular guy to wear colored contacts lenses. For a man to get away with that he'd have to be on stage, wearing a velvet, purple, pirate jacket with permed hair, eyeliner and singing *Raspberry Beret*. On Prince anything is acceptable. Just as I was trying not to judge his fake eyes, I noticed that his car had a large crack in the windshield like the kind of crack that might shatter if we hit a bump. Logically I asked him what happened. He told me some inexplicable story that had to do with poker and putting a swivel chair in his car. He also nonchalantly said he had no plans to get it fixed. Again I was trying to reserve judgment, but as women when we get into a man's car, we ask ourselves is this a car that we'd feel safe and comfortable getting into again? Is this a car we could make out in? And if we're under the age of thirty or older and we just have a moment when passion overtakes us, we ask ourselves is this a car I could have sex in? My answer was a resounding no. So we started making small talk and I asked him why we had to be at the premiere so early. He said he didn't know, but his friend who got us the tickets, told him to show up at 4pm.

Once we got settled into the cracked windshield car, I started asking him basic get to know you questions. Mind you these weren't interrogation questions. I wasn't shining a light on his face, removing his fingernails with pliers, or asking him to reveal his deepest, darkest most warped thoughts, but he was defensive and vague with every innocuous question. I asked him where he was from. His answer: "All over." "All over where?" I asked. "The continental United States?" "Just kind of all over. Mostly the West, we moved around a lot." He said finally relenting and giving me a smaller geographic region. I began to wonder if this man was in some sort of witness protection program. This was beginning to seem like a "Molly, you in danger girl" kind of moment. And I didn't even have my Mace with me because I was carrying my black Coach clutch that was fashionable, but not spacious. So I followed up with another benign question. "Was your dad in the military, is that why you moved a lot?" "My dad?!" His response was angry, verging on rage, defensive and had me thinking *this Negro is crazy and I may have to jump out of a moving vehicle.* "I have no idea who my dad is! My dad could be president of the United States for all I know," he barked. Now this was 2006 and the President was George W. Bush and my date was quite black. And I didn't think W had an interracial love child, but if he did and it was this guy I was in trouble. No Mace, in a moving vehicle with someone who becomes unhinged when one asks a simple, innocent question.

Obviously this guy had some serious daddy baggage issues, but what did I expect? My manager's vetting process was only slightly less efficient than the one used for Sarah Palin. I started to replay some of my self-defense moves in my head in case I needed them later. At this point with the fake green eyes, the busted window, the daddy issues and the witness protection program like answers, all I was looking forward to was the movie premiere. I even entertained the idea of perhaps meeting someone else at the movie premiere after party.

We arrived at Hollywood and Highland near the movie theater. The area was a frenzy, with fans, media etc. There were literally hundreds of people standing by waiting to see Tom Cruise. There was a particularly large crowd of folks across the street from where we arrived. They were all wearing Power 106FM t-shirts. My date wasn't quite sure where we were supposed to go so he started to call his friend who he said was already in the theater saving us seats. While he tried to get his friend on the phone, I watched as other premiere goers, carrying a piece of paper with information, showed their paper to a police officer who directed them across the street. I told my date that I think we should follow those people. We approached the officer, but my date didn't have any paperwork to present so he called his friend. While he was on the phone, he started waving to a person in the Power 106FM crowd.

He hung up the phone. "So we don't exactly have tickets to the movie premiere," he said. "You see that guy over there waving?" He asked. "That's my friend. Since we don't have tickets we're going to have to wait in line with all those people, but we can't wait in the front of the line with my friend. We have to wait in line over there," he said. Then he pointed to a line that stretched around the corner and beyond, I think, all the way to Santa Barbara. I wasn't sure, but it was long. Then he added, "And even if we wait in line, we might not get in. And by the way the movie doesn't start until 7:30pm." It was 4:30pm. Then my date started walking towards the end of that interminable line. I did not move. "Hold up," I said. "You expect me to wait in line for three hours and wear a Power 106 t-shirt? I don't even know what Power 106 is. I am a grown woman and someone's mother. I'm not waiting in line. You need to take me home. Now." I snapped. Then that fool had the nerve to act dejected. He said he was really looking forward to seeing that movie. Well I was really looking forward to having a date with a grown-up not someone who half-assed some plans and expected me to stand in line like some tween-ager waiting with a mob of others to catch a glimpse of the Biebs, while donning swag from Power 106. I got my hair done, shaved my legs and was paying a babysitter, but not for this bullshit. When this fake green-eyed monster didn't offer any alternative plan, or apology, or anything, I reiterated that this so-called date was over and he needed to take me home. Now! "You can come back and wait in line with your little friend, but you will be taking me home first," and yes I did say, "little friend." As if things couldn't get worse, my so-called date had the nerve to complain that he was going to have to pay for parking. He suggested we go across the street to get our parking validated at the movie theater. *How are we going to get our parking ticket validated when you didn't even have a movie ticket, you cheap, ass, motherfella?* I thought that in my head, but did not say it out aloud. I still wanted the ride home, which was the least he could do after this dating disaster and after losing this hour or so from my life, I certainly wasn't going to lose money on cab fare. My date couldn't get off the parking thing. I snatched the ticket out of his miserly hand and marched it into Sephora, where they validated it for me. As we walked to his car I was silent, but Jeff thought this was the right time to sexually proposition me. Well, it was the end of the date, which is usually the time these things happen, but how could this guy even think he was getting any sex off of me? He was delusional, but that made sense because he also believed we had tickets to the *Mission Impossible 3* movie premiere. He started complimenting me, but they were backhanded compliments. He said, "Your body looks really good for a mother." Yes, he did say that and glared at my ass while saying it. At this point, I was contemplating using one of my self-defense moves just to knock some sense into the brotha, which would have been more of an act of kindness on this empty-headed soul than a means for me to exact my frustration, but I didn't want to mess up my manicure, so I rolled my eyes at his comment, which is universal code for shut the front door. As we approached the parking attendant at the exit, Jeff put his validated ticket into the machine and the attendant said, "That will be two dollars, sir." "I thought it was validated?" He retorted. The attendant, whose nametag read, "Manuel," explained that it's two dollars with validation. My date, Jeff, started complaining to the parking attendant about the high cost of parking and our short stay in the parking structure and how it was highway robbery to charge us, but Manuel was not hearing it. In that moment Manuel and I shared a look. I shook my head and rolled my eyes at my date. Manuel communicated empathy for me and I started to wonder what if I had gone on a date with Manuel instead of this trifilin' loser who was haggling over two dollars. I bet Manuel would have actually gotten tickets to the *Mission Impossible 3* premiere or at least had an alternate plan. And I know he wouldn't have complained about the cost of parking. Before my date reluctantly removed his wallet, he had the audacity to look in my direction. Did he want me to pay half of the two whole dollars for parking? I looked at him like the fool he was. He opened his wallet and there was only three dollars in it. He gave two of them to the attendant and demanded a receipt. Yes, a receipt for the date that never was and for the two dollars that he protested paying. Then he finally took me home. When he dropped me off I told him, "Thanks, I guess." Do you know that triflin' Negro called me for two weeks afterwards assuming I'd go out with him again? I never returned his calls. The reason I cannot remember his real name is because whenever I refer to that ridiculous date I always call him: Power 106. And to this day I have not seen *Mission Impossible 3*.

Date A Homeless Guy

Many of us go on coffee first dates because we think they are quick, easy and less committal than a dinner type of situation, but one can still get a sense of who their date is. My friend Sandra has had her share of coffee first dates. On one date in particular, she met a man in Santa Monica. Now Santa Monica is an area with a high homeless population. Sandra's coffee date went well. He was a nice enough guy, but when they left the coffee house is when he showed his true, blue, un-chivalrous colors.

As they left the establishment it was dark. Sandra's car was parked in a nearby alley. The guy hugged her goodbye and as she walked down the alley, he turned to walk in the other direction and a homeless man yelled after him, "You can't even walk her to her car, man. Walk her to her car. Be a man." Sandra's coffee date laughed off the chider of the homeless man and walked away. As Sandra walked to her car, the homeless man said, "I'd walk you to your car, if you were my date. Don't worry, I'll watch after you and make sure you're safe." Sandra told him thank you and never forgot his act of chivalry. Even though the homeless man may have lost his worldly dignity of a job, a home, and even some of his teeth, he could still find the time to leave his shopping cart idle and exhibit true character by walking my friend to her car. Her date should have taken some cues from the homeless man. Sandra never went on another date with the coffee guy and she never forgot the kindness and reminder that chivalry is not dead from the homeless man.

Dating and the NBA

I interviewed a professional NBA referee for a potential television project. He told me that sometimes the refs treat the players like children. They have to set boundaries and lines that they don't allow the players to cross. Early on in games they call a lot of fouls and tighten the reigns at the start to set a precedent so the players will know how to act. The refs want them to know that if they don't behave well, they will get thrown out of the game.

As women, we need to treat romantic relationships like basketball games and act like professional referees. When you're out on a first date with a guy you've met online or anywhere and he asks you something incredibly inappropriate like, "Do you suck dick," he should get ejected from the game of dating for being a lascivious loser. Obviously this man has had no home-training. He should be forever banned from the game of dating like Pete Rose is banned from baseball. There's no chance for redemption here. If you meet a first date at a restaurant, but he offers to take you to a second location in his car, you need to call a foul. And I hope you brought your Mace, girl. If a first date tries to make his way into your apartment with some lame excuse like he needs to charge his phone, catch the ESPN highlights or use your bathroom, remind him he has not been invited up and recommend he take a leak in the bushes. If he continues to insist on coming into your place anyway, then automatically give him a foul and bench his triflin', sorry ass. First dates are supposed to be on good behavior so imagine what his bad behavior is like.

If you're in a relationship with a guy and he's not acting right, apply the NBA referee rules on him too. When your man shows up habitually late, gets texts from another woman while he's with you, uses you as a taxi service, doesn't pay attention to your needs in bed, doesn't do anything special for your birthday, he should get a foul for each offense. Once he gets six of those then he's fouled out of the game. Send him to the lockers. It's the end of the relationship road for him.

The truth is we will stop settling for bad behavior, neglect, abuse and cheating, when we feel as if we're truly worthy of something better. No one can give you self-esteem, but yourself. So dig deep and find self love first before you try to find love with someone else.

Irregular Sweaters and Effed Up Men

My friend, Tricia, went to college near some outlet stores. These stores sold Gap and Banana Republic clothing at major discounts, oftentimes because some of the clothes were irregular. It was located right by the actual factory. This was back in the late 80's when there were still manufacturing jobs in this country. The store was only open on weekends. People would line up and they'd open the doors and rabid consumers would swarm the tables, shelves and bins for deals. Imagine the lines and crowds and consumer fervor that you'd see the first day Jason Woo's designs went on sale at Target. That was the setting. Well Tricia, her roommates and I crossed the Ohio border into Kentucky to go to this Gap factory outlet store. They opened the doors and we pounced on the merchandise. I quickly found myself in a tug of war with another woman over an irregular Gap sweater. She had one sleeve and I had the other. I looked into her eyes and she looked into mine. Neither one of us was going to give way. This was proving to be more competitive than merging onto the 405 freeway on a late Friday afternoon (or really any afternoon because too many damn people live in Los Angles and don't carpool). Anyway, I tugged again and she tugged right back. It was primal and without words. Both of us had marked the territory of this medium sized, wool-blend, striped, pullover and only one of us was going to take home this kill. But then something happened. I remembered that this sweater I was in a territorial war over was irregular. So I was fighting over something that wasn't even worth it.

In that moment, I realized I wanted a sweater that wasn't irregular and I wasn't going to just take the first thing I saw out of fear that I might not find something else. I gave myself the gift of hope that there was a better sweater out there for me and I let go. Mostly I let go because I also noticed the other woman was missing a tooth. We were in Kentucky and I know from my vast experience watching *Coal Miner's Daughter* that down in Butcher Holler dental hygiene is not a priority, at least not as much as moonshine and singing around a trashcan fire. But there was a real possibility that this woman could have lost a tooth in another outlet shopping scuffle and since I liked my teeth a lot more than that mediocre sweater, I let go. The presumed Butcher Holler woman gladly snatched it away and left to continue her scavenging.

As women we are often fighting over the male equivalents of irregular sweaters and then we make excuses for those irregular men because we're desperate or lonely or believed in that J*erry Maguire* "You complete me" bullshit.

Expect The Best

So now that I talked about how to fight against the bad behavior, I think there's something else we as women can do to change our attitude in dating... expect more. In Cameron Crowe's 1992 film *Singles*, one of his characters joins a dating service and its slogan is: expect the best. Why is it that we don't expect the best when dating? So many girlfriends have said to me that they've met a great guy, but they're just waiting for the other shoe to drop. They're practically waiting for him to be a jerk. Have we been conditioned by society and *Sex and the City* to have low dating expectations? Has the statistical shortage of males in college and seemingly the world forced us to settle for irregular men? Or is it just our negative attitude that needs to change? Are we projecting negativity onto something that has the potential to be positive?

The slogan for Kohl's department store is: expect great things. So that's what we do. We expect great things when it comes to inexpensive clothing at Kohl's. I've been to

Kohl's during the holidays when things are picked over and in disarray. Despite the busyness of the department store that often times makes me nauseous and dizzy (there's something about the fluorescent lights, wafts of discounted perfume samples floating through the airspace and crying babies that practically sends me into a panic attack) and despite being in the midst of heart palpitating panic, I have still been able to find a gem of clothing during the frenzy of the season at Kohl's without Xanax. So their slogan holds up and I think we should adopt that for life. We expect to get a Vera Wang design at an affordable price. Why not expect to find a good man? With men we don't have that expectation, so we know we're going to get shit and we prepare for it. Then we prepare to fix the guy and the relationship instead of expecting someone and something great when we get it. I mean, isn't that what we all want, but are too afraid to ask for? Who wants a mediocre love life? We may not admit that out in front of everyone, but that's what we expect and we plan for, I mean, if we got great, then what would we complain about to our girlfriends, our waxing ladies, or to the random woman we meet in the ladies' room? There is kinship in complaining about our men so perhaps we enjoy the community that having a lousy husband/boyfriend creates for us. If we expected great men and relationships what would women's magazines write about? We'd no longer see articles warning us that our man is cheating, will have erectile dysfunction, or won't ever propose. *Cosmo* would no longer be able to scare us into sexual gymnastic tricks (that can cause back spasms... I heard) that we need to do to keep our relationship hot. Our society tells us to live in fear, that we're going to lose our man or never get one unless we buy this dress, get this haircut, that Brazilian wax and try these seven new bedroom moves.

A Dater's Bill Of Rights

1. You have the right to decline an invitation from a guy who asks you out for the first time via text and the text contains horrifically misspelled third grade words, unless you're in the third grade then why the heck are you dating and texting?
2. You have the right to decline a same day invitation, if it's a first date.
3. You have the right to turn around and go home if the guy you're meeting for a coffee date cannot open the door for you, pay for your cup of coffee or walk you to your car.
4. You have the right to turn around and go home if the guy you have met over the internet and are now meeting in person for the first time has obviously used a fake photo or photoshopped his real photo and in no

way resembles his online profile picture. This man is a liar, delusional or he's impersonating someone.
5. You have the right to turn down a first date invitation when the guy cannot make an actual plan for the date. If he is so indecisive and asks you out without any clue about where he wants to take you or how much money he wants to spend and leaves the decision making to you, then this guy may not actually have any balls. If you do accept his non-invitation and you make a plan for the date, you basically just asked yourself out and planned your own date. You don't need him for that.
6. You have the right to never take another call from a man who has set up a date with you, but then calls a few hours before to cancel and his reason for canceling is that he has to clean his house, or a similarly triflin' excuse.
7. Your Tinder Date tracks you down at a candlelight vigil. It is there that he thinks it's appropriate to meet for the first time. You have the right to ignore that triflin' bastard, or just left swipe him to his face.

Some of the aforementioned scenarios happened to me and to dear friends of mine. I was a victim of scenario number one. The guy was younger than me so I let my no first date text invitation rule slide. I didn't want to discriminate against his education so I also excused his poor spelling and grammar until it got to the point where the spelling was so horrific that it didn't resemble English anymore. I realized that my second grade son's spelling and grammar were better than this guy's.

Inappropriate First Date Stories and Opening Lines

1. When a guy begins the date by telling you his ex-wife left him for a guy with a Jheri Curl and it's 2015, there's probably no future with this man.
2. When your first date mentions during appetizers that the last person he dated gave him HPV, you shouldn't bother waiting for the main course.
3. When your date tells you he hasn't paid taxes in seven years, make sure you have cab fare home, girl, because he may get arrested before the date ends.

The Top Ten Most Inexcusable Behavior Moves

If your man fits any one of these, then get your ass out, like right now. I mean drop everything, but the book. Hold onto the book 'cause you're going to need that, but if you're holding a skillet, drop that preferably on his head. If you're on the toilet, stop in mid-stream and get out of the house. If you're having sex, get your ass off of that triflin' Negro, redneck, machismo Latino, Armenian motherfella, you're living with, married to, or dating. Just get out, girl! Run. Now if he's in your house pack up his shit and serenade him with the lyrics of Beyoncé's song, "Irreplaceable." She was nice enough to put his crap in a box. I'd just throw it on the curb, but that's me.

Real Life Examples of Bad Behavior

1. You're at a cocktail party with a date, or your boyfriend, and he asks you to go fetch him a drink so that he can continue his conversation with another woman.
2. Your husband doesn't want you to attend your Grandmother's funeral because you have not been able to arrange a babysitter for your children. It's your Grandmomma. She's only going to die once. They're his kids too!
3. Your man asks to borrow money early on in the relationship. Do not lend or give money to any man who is not a blood relative and over the age of 16.
4. When you go to pick up your engagement ring, his credit card gets turned down and he looks to you to pay for the balance, promising he'll pay you back. Number one: do you want to buy your own engagement ring? If you do, you're really just proposing to yourself. The

diamond industry has already marketed right hand rings for single girls. You can go get one of those without his dumb ass. Please know that if you marry him, moments after you endure twenty-seven hours of hard labor delivering his child, and the hospital asks who will be taking care of the bill, he will hand it over to you. So get ready to write a check during your episiotomy.

5. He reveals to you that he has a non-curable sexually transmitted disease after you've already had sex. Or, you finally have sex with a guy after being abstinent for a year. Soon afterwards you break out in blisters down there. When you try to confront the asshole, he doesn't return your calls.
6. He gets a 2am booty call from a guy.
7. After you've dated for several months you find out he has a girlfriend. He tells you that his having a girlfriend is no one's business. Well, it's your business when you catch an STD from that fool and his girlfriend. It's your business because he's now unwittingly made you the other woman.
8. He's your boyfriend, but also your sister's husband. Both of you are really at fault here.
9. You have cancer and are staying in a cancer treatment center that is just for patients, but your man is so triflin' that he's gotten himself or the both of you evicted while you're sick with cancer. So he moves into the treatment

center with you because he's basically homeless, but you aren't because you have cancer. The center gets wind of your man's scam. You both get kicked out. So now the two of you are homeless and guess what? You still have cancer. At this point, I'm not sure what's worse: the malignant tumor eating away at your major organs or the triflin' asshole boyfriend/ husband you've invited into your life.

10. You're on your honeymoon. Your husband keeps getting calls from another woman. He actually takes the calls. And the woman is not his mother, sister or auntie calling with some life-threatening emergency. She's a "friend" who needs him right now.

BONUS

11. It's always about him. Everything is always about him. If you have gotten fired, lost a limb or your mother died, your boyfriend/husband/boo thing somehow makes the tragic event about him, or whatever he's going through eclipses your tragedy so you end up taking care of him. This is a man with a character disorder called NARCISSISM. Yes, he may have been charismatic, charming and interested in you when you first met him, but now when you don't pay enough attention to

him or things don't go his way, he's prone to rages. He never admits to wrongdoing. His disease is incurable. As one learned psychiatrist told me, narcissism is the worst mental illness. Even schizophrenics have some awareness that they are crazy, but narcissists never will. If you are with this kind of man, I will pray for you, girl. My advice is to hit the ejection button from this relationship immediately, if not sooner. Seriously, get your parachute ready and jump out of the plane like a fighter pilot who is about to be gunned down by the enemy because staying with this particular kind of jerk will just be a prolonged war that can never be won.

If your man exhibits any of this behavior, do not pass go for a second date or even couples counseling. The only possible excuse for the kind of behavior I described in my top 11 list is that the man is brain-injured and by dating him you're fulfilling some sort of charity/community service work. So unless a brain injury is involved, your man just told you or showed you who he is and that's not changing because we cannot change men. They are usually on their best behavior while dating so this is as good as it gets with this motherfella. Make sure you bring cab money, girl. But, believe there are better guys out there too.

CHAPTER THREE
Dick Is Not An Endangered Species

Desperation and loneliness can lead to poor dating decisions. Sometimes as women, we feel it's better to be on the bottom of some guy's roster than not be on any rosters at all. We degrade ourselves and respond to men who make farm animal noises to get our attention on the street. We must stop thinking and acting like dick is an endangered species.

When I was a naïve college freshman, I happened to run into a cousin on an airplane. This cousin, who is older, offered me some startling words of wisdom slash advice about men and dating. Now I was a young, eighteen year-old virgin and I was stunned by the crass talk from her, but it left an indelible mark. She told me that I could get dick anywhere, so don't be too quick to give it up. What I really needed to look for was a quality man. She was right. If you think about it dick is like Starbucks. There's one on every corner. What we want and need to require are real men with integrity and character who value us. Those men are few and far between, like Peet's Coffee Houses, and often when you do find one he's married... to either a woman or, in some states, a man.

Dickfax

With all this talk about the male genitalia, there are three things that are of the utmost importance regarding sex: intel, background checks and STD tests. As women, we need to get more information about the men we let into our lives and our va-jay–jays. Several years ago, I bought a new car. Before I bought the car, I did extensive research. I considered buying a used car because I could get the Carfax on the used vehicle. I could find out how many owners it had before me, the maintenance record and information about any accidents. Well ladies, we need to get the Carfax on dicks or as I like to call it: Dickfax. We need an Internet database with the history of the dick. What previous owners or users have to say about it; how many children it has fathered; how many STD's it has had; does it have bad credit? This isn't something E-harmony offers in their full profile of prospective dates. We need to create this. There is something intrinsically wrong with the fact that we know more about the previously owned vehicle we're driving than the used penis that we're riding. We need to get boots on the ground and start a movement, a coalition and involve our international sisters too. Go global with the Dickfax.

The bottom line is sex should not be an impulse purchase. Chastity isn't dead, but it certainly needs a revival. Short of that, we should at least be more informed penile users.

Hardball Dating

To get the more that we deserve we need to ask men the tough questions just like MSNBC's Chris Matthews does on *Hardball*. Chris is unapologetic when he puts people on blast. He's not afraid to call someone a racist or an idiot or a racist idiot. We need to channel Chris Matthews when we're just getting to know prospective suitors or better yet hire Chris Matthews to interrogate potential dates. Short of getting Chris, we need to stop asking men where they're from and what they do for a living? Start asking them if they came from an emotionally abusive home. Was your father an alcoholic? Has anyone ever described you as co-dependent? Was your mother cold and withholding? Of course we should ask these tough questions elegantly, but we shouldn't be afraid to ask and we have to be even braver to face the truth and not allow guys to joke or wiggle their way out of the uncomfortable questions. Chris Matthews bristles people. He makes them uncomfortable. It's confrontational television. In relationships we don't like to look at the ugly stuff. We like to live in fantasyland and believe that everything is all wine and roses, but if we had more of a *Hardball* attitude, then we'd get closer to the truth and reality.

Sadly, the reason we don't ask the hardball questions is we're desperate and afraid. Mostly we're afraid we'll die alone. Have you ever noticed that Life Alert commercials only feature sad, old, single women whose destiny is to die alone, but are saved from a solitary death by a button around their necks that calls a sad, single, old lady alarm center where a minimum wage worker talks the old lady through what may be her last moments on earth, as she gasps for breath from her heart attack or fall? None of us wants to be that sad, old lady who has to wear a life alert necklace and exchange her last words with a stranger who may or may not speak English as a second language. I mean, can you imagine dying and trying to decipher what your Life Alert worker is saying to you or you say your final words to the Life Alert guy, but he gets them all wrong? So when your children ask Life Alert what were mother's final words he says something like, "She say she had a duck in the pub, but could not come so help me to come. And for hell fun she loves Tim and marijuana." That was his English as a second language interpretation. What mother really said was, "I'm stuck in the tub please come help me. And tell my son I love him and Marjorie." Yes, your final words could be lost in translation because you died single, old, alone and probably naked in the bathtub, and the caring Life Alert immigrant was your final interaction with humanity. That's the great fear. And the thing is they don't feature men in those commercials. Eighty-year old men aren't afraid to die alone because there's some old widow around the corner who, despite her arthritis and fixed income will sacrifice her social security payments and nearly paralyzed hands to care for this man hoping that he won't outlive her so she doesn't have to get a Life Alert necklace.

We're all still suffering from the hangover of a generation of mothers who were defined by being wives and mothers. Many parents still regard marriage and procreation (some parents are still holding out for the procreation to come after the marriage) as real success for their daughters. As women, we need to live our own dreams and not try to adhere to some sort of picket fence societal, parental dream for our future or because Life Alert commercials instill fear.

It's not just our mothers, pop culture and E-harmony all put an inordinate amount of pressure on us as single women. I love, adore and worship at the stage of Beyoncé, but even her hit song "Single Ladies" wasn't as empowering as she thinks because I've been in a situation when, "I had gloss on my lips and had squeezed my hips into some really tight jeans, but he still didn't like it enough to put a ring on it," and when he saw me again, he wasn't mad because no one else was trying to put a ring on it either. I was still single and alone. And a few months later he put a ring on someone else. So there, Beyoncé. Go create a song out of that, which I'm sure she will and probably sell millions of records. Single is not the enemy, but it can feel awfully lonely on a Saturday night when you see your ex with someone else or long to be with a guy who looks right past you.

And E-harmony and other online dating company's commercials are especially vicious. Their advertisements are like Disney ads for kids. Disney both entices and terrifies little children by dangling the carrot of a coveted DVD of *Pinnochio* or *Cinderella*, but then the ads tell them in an ominous voice-over that if those kids don't yell and scream and demand that their parents buy them that DVD right NOW it's going away in the vault, which is like a dungeon, and will never be seen again. Online dating websites do the same thing. They buy ad space on lonely Saturday nights and run their propaganda during commercial breaks of movies like: *When Harry Met Sally*, or basically any other 90's movie with Meg Ryan where she had a cute hair cut. The dating commercials tell you that your soul mate is out there waiting for you, but if you don't sign up this weekend he'll be taken. Maybe he'll be taken into a vault too. I guess the grown-up version of a vault would be a dungeon. The point is your soul mate is in someone else's sex dungeon and not yours so you're a fool because you didn't sign up and you're still single. Maybe you're eligible for a discounted Life Alert necklace?

Repairs For One

I'm single and have been so for a while. A loooooong while. In fact, a few years ago I reached a really low point in my singledom. My showerhead was malfunctioning and not because I was using it for anything other than bathing. It's not detachable anyway. The nozzle wasn't functioning properly so my showers had turned into dribbles of water. I called my homeowners insurance policy and they referred me to a repairman. He was Russian and let's call him Leo because I don't remember his name and also because I'm a Tolstoy fan. Leo examined my shower. In his thick Russian accent he began to explain the problem to me. He started off with, "Is easy to fix." Don't all repairmen begin sentences that way, especially if they are not going to fix it themselves? And by the way it should be easy for you to fix, Leo. You have a degree in plumbing whereas I have a degree in cinema. So unless I'm going to make a movie about my showerhead, my knowledge of Italian Neorealism is useless in this situation as it is in almost every other real life situation. Thank you Mom and Dad for paying for USC School of Cinema.

Leo launched into his do-it-yourself tutorial and watched my eyes glaze over. He stopped himself and said, "If you can't do it, do you have husband?" I gave my stock answer,

"Not anymore." Not anymore always gives people pause. I guess they're wondering what anymore means. Does it mean I simply divorced him, or did he somehow meet his demise-- and by my blithe, sardonic intonation, I think people wonder if I helped him meet his demise. Anyway, Leo didn't miss a beat. After he discovered I didn't have a husband, he asked, "Do you have boyfriend?" Leo hit me below the belt with this one. I was vulnerable, dateless and unable to bathe properly for the last week. Explaining my convoluted dating status to a man for whom English is a second language seemed like a colossal waste of time. The bottom line is the guy who had been sending me vague text messages for weeks and the other guy, who I made out with in a bar twice, were not good candidates to help me fix my showerhead. I answered forlornly, "No." Leo read the pain in my eyes and tried to make me feel better by responding, "Oh, I am so sorry for you. No husband. No boyfriend. Too bad." His condemnation about my marital status was actually worse than my mother's. In that moment, I wished that I had some witty, Carrie Bradshaw retort that adroitly proclaimed my singledom pride, but singles don't have pride-boasting chants, at least nothing that rolls off the tongue like: *I'm here, I'm queer get used to it*, which is catchy, but not applicable in my case. Gay people are so lucky. They have the cool slogans that rhyme.

So Leo went on to say, "Well, I tell you how to fix your shower because insurance no cover this." As a single female homeowner I bought this insurance policy to bail me out in situations just like this one. I pay a monthly premium so that I can have a repairman at my beck and call and also because I'm intimidated by Home Depot. Now not only was my insurance not going to help me, my repairman pities me for being an old maid. I didn't need this crap. I just wanted a nice, warm shower. I listened intently as Leo explained how I could buy some sort of tool to fix my shower myself. And I assured him that I completely understood what to do and didn't need a man. I didn't even need him, or my useless insurance policy that clearly discriminated against me because I'm do-it-yourself/repair challenged.

As soon as Leo left, did I do as he had instructed me: get the tools to fix my shower, prove him wrong and exact my feminism on this entire situation? No. I did what any God-fearing, tragically single girl would do. I got right on that Internet and finally finished my E-harmony application, which by the way was more involved than my mortgage application, but I guess that makes sense because Wells Fargo was only promising me a 30-year loan at a fixed rate, while E-harmony was offering me a lifetime of love. At this point, I wasn't even seeking love or companionship. I just wanted a nice guy to have around the house to fix things and tell me I looked pretty. I sent my dating profile off into cyberspace and waited for someone to poke, wink or friend me. Today my house is worth a lot less than what I paid for it seven years ago and I never got one date out of E-harmony, but I did fix my shower all by myself. I didn't even use the tool Leo recommended. I used my fingernail. So I didn't need a man after all. But later, I did need a manicure.

Housework

I met a man at a party. We exchanged information and he called me a few days later. We played a little phone tag, but then we finally spoke. Our conversation was great and long. Finally, at the end of the conversation we got around to talking about what we were doing for the weekend and he said we should get together. He didn't distinctively ask me out with a formal plan, but we decided to go out on Sunday night. He called me late Sunday afternoon to cancel our date. He cited the fact that he had to clean his house as his reason. He was going out of the country in a few days and his house was a mess so he needed to clean it before he left. Yes, that happened. A man chose cleaning his house over me. I had never felt so slighted. From then on I nicknamed this guy: Housework. And that should have been the end of my interaction with him, but I excused his behavior. I rationalized that since he was leaving the country, perhaps there was cause to clean. I knew in my heart and my gut that this was a pitiful excuse and I am a gem, who he should not dismiss, but due to my lack of dates, bad luck in love and P.T.D.D, I told him to have a good trip and he said he'd call when he got back.

He did call when he returned and we spoke at length about his trip overseas, but I was surprised that by the end of the conversation, he did not ask me out again. I wondered what was really going on with Housework. Some time passed and he called again. We spoke at length, but again he did not ask me out. I then began to consult my expert panel of girlfriends. These are my sisters who have studied men and dating since our tween years and have developed theories, philosophies and interpretations for male/dating behavior. My friend Liz spelled it out for me harshly. "This guy doesn't really like you," she said. "The truth is that he's probably seeing other women and he is trying to keep you on the back burner in case he ever wants to go out with you or sleep with you." Her words stung. I felt acid start to burn in my stomach as I digested this cold, hard truth. Basically this guy, Housework, was keeping me on his roster of women. I was his back burner booty. You know the pot you keep on the stove to warm up and then serve later, that's what I was to Housework. His periodic calls were his turning up the burner to keep me warm, but he never had any intention of calling me off the bench to actually play. At that time in my life I didn't have a lot of male attention. I did enjoy talking to Housework, but I still didn't understand why he never asked me out. It almost became a game. With every phone call I kept thinking Housework would certainly ask me out during this conversation. It never happened.

Finally his calls stopped, but then I ran into him at a party. We talked a bit, but again he did not make any plans with me. He wasn't with another woman at the party. I left thinking I'd never hear from him again, but alas he called. By this point I understood my position on his roster and like the Nike slogan says, *play me or trade me*. I told Housework I could not just keep talking to him on the phone. I don't need another friend to gab with. So unless he wanted to make plans, I had to go. He didn't make plans, nor did he ever call again. So I was never called up from the D league to play for Housework's team. I've grown so much since my brief non-liaison with Housework. I know now that when a man chooses dirty dishes, trash and vacuuming over me, he is not deserving of me. And even if he lied and "housework" was his cover story, I deserved a more creative, thoughtful excuse.

Swine Calls

Have you ever been on the street and a man, be it a construction worker, gardener, usually a man with a tool belt will call out to you? I'm sure the answer is yes. It's a rite of passage for women like getting your period, or a bad perm. Both make you feel shitty for about a week. But those catcalls from construction men make you feel somewhere between shitty, hot, victimized, concerned about your safety and totally offended. I've passed by workmen and have heard whistles, catcalls and yells. While living in London, the men were well mannered. They didn't whistle or yell. One man simply said, "Hello, love" to me in a dreamy, proper British accent and smiled.

In Paris, the men were more forward. Even out of Paris, the French men I've encountered are more forward. Years ago while in France, I was strolling down the Avenue des Champs-Élysées with my mother, when a French man stopped me and asked if I'd like to go home with him. This was my first trip to Paris and I actually couldn't believe this man was asking me the cliché phrase from the song "Lady Marmalade" "Voulez Vous Couche Avec Moi Ce Soir?" I mean, I didn't even need my three years of high school French and subsequent two years of college French for translation of this because I was familiar with the Patti LaBelle hit. That night on the street in Paris was another one of those moments when I half expected a camera crew to come out of the woodwork and say, "We got you." You're on the French version of candid camera, but alas this guy was serious. To his credit he was inclined to go anywhere and not just his place, but his intention was clear he wanted me and sex would ensue. I was perplexed because I wasn't even dressed like a hooker. In fact, I think I was wearing a turtleneck. It was a cold May evening. When I explained to him in my best college French III that I was with my mother,

"Je sui avec ma mere." He simply said he didn't care. Ew! He just wanted to go somewhere with me. I repeated that I was with my mother and I didn't know him, but thanks for the offer. My mother and I walked away. He called after me, but I ignored him. First of all I had no business thanking him for his offer to take me off the street and back to his place so he could screw me, but I was thrown because I'm an American. And the American equivalent of the European pick up line is a whistle, catcall or a pig call. So at least the European men actually spoke to me as a human being, while American men whistle and make obscene noises at me as if I'm a dog on the street. The worst offense was when a man whistled at me then made a sound that I can only liken to a swine call. Yes, a man called me like a farmer would call his pigs. If any woman responds to a swine call, she is likening herself to a pig going to the troth. Troths are nasty, disease-ridden and full of backwash, which is what I imagine is a similar make-up to the man who gave the swine call. Is that what we want for ourselves as women?

Thunder Down Under

The only respectable places for women to whistle, scream and completely objectify men are male revue strip clubs like Chip 'n' Dales, *Magic Mike* or Thunder Down Under in Vegas. This male objectification takes place in a controlled environment where men have chosen to put themselves and their bodies out there for public consumption. But here is the catch. Men have monetized their sexual degradation better than women. As women we put up with the catcalls, pig calls and whistles everyday in the street and we don't make a dime off of it. Those dudes at Thunder Down Under are making a salary, plus tips AND those motherfellas have dental. We all know women are better tippers than men so the Thunder Down Under strippers are doing fine. They also don't have to worry about getting raped after work on their way to their car. I'm not advocating selling sex at all. As women we just need to take our power back and that begins with demanding respect from all men and especially those strangers in the street who think they can call us like farm animals and get a response.

Again I reference the Carrie Underwood song "Before he Cheats" because she made an important point. She will not be cheated on again, but there's a girl around the corner who is willing to put up with some man's triflin' ways. There is a girl next door with low self-esteem who thinks she's nothing without a man even if he's a loser. She is willing to pick up your loser, that you have put on the curb like a used up old couch piece of trash, and call that asshole a treasure which is why there are so many men out there with no jobs, raggedy cars, lazy, drunk, abusive, philandering losers who are still making hog calls to women on the street because some woman responded positively to the pig call. She gave out her number. She went on a date, and she had sex with the pig caller. So why should he change his act? Why should he be respectful of women, get a job, stop drinking and cheating when it works for him? People continue to act a certain way because it's usually proved to be beneficial. Dr. Phil always asks people what's the payoff for your behavior? Lazy, raggedy, philandering losers don't change because their bad behavior has lured many a woman into their triflin' lairs.

Nicknames I've given dates or boyfriends

1. Power 106
2. Housework
3. Uncomfortably large penis guy (Yes, because it was too big and there is such a thing.)
4. Raspberry Beret (Because a guy I met on J-Date made the choice to wear one without ever referencing Prince.)
5. Why Doesn't He Love Me Guy a.k.a heartbreak hotel, shattered dreams and the guy I wasted my youth on so now I'm old and alone.

CHAPTER FOUR

They Shoot 40-Year Old Women Don't They?

It seems like the Internet and every other episode of *Dr. Oz* tells me how hard it is to lose weight after 40. Well, I know something even more challenging: dating after 40. Many of us dating in our 40's never thought we'd be here because we got married when we were supposed to, in our 20's and 30's, but the marriages didn't work out, or the husband died so we're left to raise children as single or divorced moms, provide for a family, and date. I know what you're thinking if you've hit your middle forties. That age, 45, should come with a warning label because it's as if overnight you've gained weight, gone blind and started losing your hair. So now you're supposed to find a date while you're fat, blind and bald. And all the fat, blind and bald 40-year old men aren't looking at you. Dating after 40 can be a cruel adventure, but you've made it this far in life so why not keep the adventure going?

If you've just begun the dating game again the rules have changed. Your smartphone is now your Yenta and she has apps for every dating site known to man, woman and transgender. It's daunting. It's dangerous. You should look into the HPV vaccine for yourself, not just your teenage daughter. It is not a desperate situation. You can do it. You're not alone. In fact, there are plenty of other 40 something women who are your direct competition or allies depending on how you look at it. It's important to continue to value yourself and look at your age as an advantage. Just because you're over 40 doesn't mean you've entered into a new dating category: old, desperate and lonely. I know 40-year old women who would hang out in an Ebola ward if they heard there was an available, attractive, male doctor they could meet and date. Don't be that girl. Rather don't be that middle-aged woman.

Desperation is real and I get it. Maybe it's been so long since you had a sexual experience that you go buy a copy of the *Fellatio For Dummies* book (I don't think that exists. I just made it up, but maybe I should write it, though I lack expertise in that area). While it's nice to brush up on your skills, do not try out your new technique on the next fool you right swipe on Tinder because you're lonely and out of practice.

Maybe you're over 40 and want a baby so bad that when you get to hold one and smell its head, you actually begin to lactate. Perhaps you've even had your eggs frozen, but they're getting old. So you have old, frozen eggs that at this point have freezer burn and there's no man in the picture to even think about thawing them out for so you just grab up whichever joker doesn't look like a sociopath on the subway so you can make a baby before your old eggs go bad.

I know women who are getting older and think that because they don't have the body of a 22 year-old, they have to settle for what they can get in the boyfriend department. That is a lie. Just because my boobs aren't as high as they used to be doesn't mean I have to settle for a loser who doesn't treat me right. Your boobs may be lower, but that doesn't mean your standards should be lower too. Get a good bra and raise them both. Don't be an over 40 desperate, old and lonely dater. Be an over 40 wise, confident and discerning dater.

Buying Jeans and Dating After 40

Dating over 40 and shopping for jeans are both essentially the same exercise... in humiliation. I do have hope that we can have better experience in both arenas, but to date that hasn't happened. You begin both exercises with a sense of dread because the jean pool and dating pool after the age of 40 have diminished. Shopping for jeans and dating over age 40 are not for the faint of heart, nor are they quick excursion to finding what you want the first time you search. When you were 20 you could meet a guy anywhere: in college, at a bar, on the street, doing laundry, at the gym, at the store, while breathing. After the age of 40, the available men-- well I don't know where the hell they are -- if I did, I'd be writing a book about that. In your 20's, you barely had to try a pair of jeans on to know they'd fit and you fit into almost every design, type, cut, style of jeans at any store. And by the way, if you're 43, that's not Forever 21 so don't shop there anymore. That mini-skirt and midriff tee you're wearing... It's embarrassing. If you have to ask yourself if you can get away with wearing it, the answer is an emphatic no. If your teenage daughter hasn't already told you yet, I'm telling you. You also need to retire your Danskins. The only grown woman who can get away with dancing around in a leotard is Beyoncé. You are not Beyoncé, you're Eileen from Peoria--I'm guessing--you're fantastic, but you're not Queen B. After the age of 40 finding the right man and the right pair of jeans that actually fit you is like a unicorn sighting. It's winning the Super Lotto of life. I'm in between men right now and two sizes away from fitting back into my skinny jeans.

 After 40 what you want in a man and jeans are similar. You just want a pair that compliment you, enhance the positive, downplay the negative and make you feel good about yourself, even sexy or cute. You want a pair of jeans that will give a little and continue to fit for many years despite how much your body changes. So in this search for the perfect pair of jeans and man, you may grow weary and even settle for something that doesn't do everything you need or want it to do. You make concessions and rationalizations with the jeans. These jeans look great on me as long as I don't sit down... or walk... or exhale. We have to buy the jeans that are right for us. Not too tight, or too youthful, or too baggy. Don't buy the ones that are in style and cost $200.00 just because they're in style and you have $200.00. Seriously, if you're going to pay a couple hundred dollars for a pair of True Religion jeans then they better be ministering to you, or performing walking on water type of miracles with your ass. I mean, making it look as firm and as round as J.Lo's kind of miracle. If not, put that $200.00 toward your real religion and into the offering basket at church. Don't buy jeans that hurt you while you wear them, or the ones you have to become a temporary anorexic to fit into, or the ones you have to do some sort of yoga pretzel move to put on your body. Buy jeans and find a man that don't require extraordinary effort, that fit into your life and style. That grow with you and support you. And don't borrow someone else's jeans and try to make them your own. Buy your own jeans and customize them if you have to. Take them in at the waist, hem them. Don't desperately hold onto an old pair, hoping they'll fit again. Take your time when looking. Try on a lot of jeans until you find the right pair that you love and love wearing... for as long as you both shall live.

Drive By Shooting of a 40yr old Woman

A few years ago I attended a movie premiere and party with a friend of mine who is an accomplished director and my sometime writing partner. We had both recently turned 40 and we weren't ashamed of it, even though we were in Los Angeles. He had even had a 40th birthday party, though the party was actually held in New York where they revere age and wisdom, not botox and *Access Hollywood*. Anyway, we watched the film and then went to the after party where the actors in the film and others mingled and partied.

An actor from a hit TV series at the time was at the party. He knew my writing partner and we were introduced. The actor, let's call him Dave, was a little flirtatious with me. My writing partner excused himself to mingle while Dave and I chatted. As our conversation continued I think Dave could tell that unlike seventy-five percent of the women there I wasn't a typical Hollywood starlet. My scope of conversation topics was not limited to my agent, my trainer or my latest audition, but unfortunately that is what gave away my age. Yes, my intelligence was my downfall in this potential dating scenario. When I mentioned to Dave I had just finished reading a book, he looked at me like I had just confessed to him I had herpes. He was quite taken aback by the fact that I read for pleasure. The most reading actors do in this town is of their sides for an audition. Yes, I'm a reader in a city where many people only watch sizzle reels and skim scripts. In the end, I believe it was my reference to Ted Kennedy's Memoir that was the nail in the coffin of any potential romance with this guy because that revealed I was of a certain age.

Dave was taken with me I could tell. Others would greet him and he would say hello, but quickly return his attention to me. Although I looked the part of the ingénue and someone who Dave could see himself with, he succumbed to his shallow Hollywood roots and asked my age. I told him to guess. So he started asking me questions like what did Bell, Biv and DeVoe mean to me. Finally I told him with pride that I had just turned 40. To which Dave responded, "Oh, I'm going to get something to eat." We were standing right by the buffet table. Dave raced away in the opposite direction of me and the food, immediately fleeing the scene as if he were escaping a burning building. I mean, he ran away from me so quickly one would have thought I had just shown him my third nipple (which I don't have). Or told him I was really a man, (which I'm not), but that may have been easier for him to digest than announcing the truth... I was 40. Dave got the hell out of there because no self-respecting television star hits on a 40-year old woman at a party. My writing partner saw the drive-by and yes, that's how quickly Dave escaped the scene of my 40-year old age revelation, like he had just shot me and was on the run from police. It was ageism at its best and worst. There was no mistaking it. I had been discriminated against sexually for my age. It was a different kind of harassment. The kind where they act like you don't exist because you're over 40. Moments later my 40 year old male writing partner could only laugh and ask me when I was going to start lying about my age.

If These Breasts Could Talk

A couple of years ago I had to see my breast surgeon who is a woman. I've had a couple of benign lumps removed from my breasts in the past, which is why I have a breast surgeon in the first place. My breasts are real, and not enhanced. They are battle scarred and war torn having been used for a year of breastfeeding. Anyway, I have a great rapport with my surgeon and of course she has intimate knowledge of my breasts. That day when I came into her office she greeted me with her usual hug and asked me about work and my love life which were both in the crapper at that time. Her response to my love life was kind of surprising. She told me rather flippantly, yet with great conviction, that men were superfluous. Now I was in her examining chair, naked from the top up and she was kneading my breasts. I think she was specifically palpating the left nipple when she said men are superfluous. So my first thought was is this some sort of sapphic statement, but it wasn't.

She had lived long enough, endured marriage and gotten to a place in her life with grown-ish children, a thriving medical practice, and supportive friends and family to recognize that out of all the facets of her life the part that was needless was that part that involved a man or men in the romantic, marriage sense. I wanted to believe her. And for five minutes I tried. I don't need a man, but I'd like one very much. Having a woman dogmatically state that men are superfluous, while she's holding my bare breast in her hands and NOT having it resonate with me just solidified my unequivocal heterosexuality. I like men to open my doors and carry my luggage. I also like them to do the dishes and drive carpool in a *Lean-In,* Sheryl Sandberg, sort of way. I like certain men to touch the small of my back, put their leg over mine in bed and be engulfed in their big broad shouldered arms. I like to look up at my man, who is taller than me and stronger than me (physically) and have him walk on the outside of the sidewalk closer to traffic. I also prefer to have a man touch my breasts than my wonderful, adorable breast surgeon. So I keep believing, dating, and looking for love. The kind of love that I want, deserve, that supports and edifies me. Yes, and I dare to keep doing this even after the age of 40.

Let's Banish The C-word: Cougar

That word is just sexist and misogynistic. Older men who pursue younger women are just called men. Yet, women who do the same have to have a name with a negative connotation. I've been hit on by much younger men. I've even gone out with a couple of younger guys, but I am not a Cougar. Look, if you're 40 or over and a younger guy wants you and you want him, you owe it to yourself and every 40-year old woman in America to see that through. Enjoy it. Experience it. Blog and Instagram about it to make us all envious. Don't demean yourself by allowing that "C" name to cross your lips about yourself or any other woman. If you find a young, hot Channing Tatum type who wants your 40 something fabulous self, you give yourself a pat on the back, girl and start calling yourself a Shero 'cause that's what you are to me.

CHAPTER FIV

You Can Change Him Girl, Is a Lie

Obviously the deep thinking, actor who discovered my age and ran like I had Ebola would never accept a woman my age. There is no changing that man. But many women believe, subscribe to, tell their friends, their daughters and the lady on the subway that any man can be trained or changed. First, we must understand that we have to accept people for who they are and not try to change them into whomever we want them to be. To possess the audacity to think one can change a person is literally a delusion of grandeur. No one is completely compatible all the time in life. Relationships go through seasons of change. If you think about your friendships, there are times that you can be very close and traveling in the same lane as a girlfriend and then there are other times that it can seem as if you're traveling on a different continent than that same friend. Ride or die's even have seasons when they aren't riding or dying for you. It isn't for us to decide to change that friend and

...d them to walk the same direction you're walking. The same is true for romantic relationships. If you're reading this and find that you're in a relationship where you are trying to change the other person so much, then perhaps that person is not the best suited match for you at this time.

I'm here to kill and bury the myth that you can train or change a man. Dogs can be trained. If you need your dog trained, call the dog whisperer, Cesar Millan. Maybe you can change the way your man dresses if you buy him a brand new wardrobe and throw all of his old clothes away. His only choice would be to run around naked or wear all the new clothes you got him. That change might work for a while. If your man does not want children, don't let your eggs rot while waiting for him to change his mind on that. If your man has told you from day one he's not interested in marriage, don't pick out China patterns hoping and praying you'll change his mind. And if he's told you he doesn't want children or to get married, certainly don't get pregnant hoping you'll force him into marriage and fatherhood. If your man likes to drink to excess a lot, do not confuse yourself with Bill W. You cannot help him. You cannot save him. There was only one savior and his name was Jesus Christ, not (insert your name here). So do not try to preach the twelve steps to him, just take one step out of the door. Move on. Michelle Obama's "Let's Move" campaign is adaptable. It's not just a program to get American children physically fit, it can be adapted to get American women to move too–move away from the big, fat, drunk loser on the couch next to you.

The alcoholic example is extreme, but I'm serious when I write about not being in the business of changing people. That's a bankrupt business. If you need your man trained to do anything beyond the spectrum of putting his dirty socks in the hamper, or dishes in the dish washer (which is something that you ask of them as a means to participate in cleaning your home, but you may not get it), if you're looking to change any sort of personality defect such as his need to look at other women whether they're live and in person or naked on the internet, then you need an act of God.

I know one philanderer who changed his ways after he was diagnosed with an inoperable brain tumor. What was truly a miraculous was the man's long-suffering wife found a brain surgeon at a notable hospital who was willing to try an experimental procedure on his brain tumor. The wife, whom he had cheated on and verbally abused over the years stood by his side. She was in fact fulfilling her "in sickness" portion of her vows to the letter. Well, her husband lived through the surgery. He is now a changed man. In fact, he's at church every Sunday and has given up his philandering. That is an act of God, ladies. You, however, are not the Lord, so if you think you can stop your man from being what he is, from denying his essence that you've tricked yourself into believing is good, but truthfully you know is down and dirty, then you are a fool. Stop yourself. Don't waste your time or energy. Don't put up with his bullshit because you think he's going to change. He can't be changed or fixed. The truth is when you get a man you're getting him as is, without a warranty. A lemon isn't one day going to magically turn into a Lamborghini. It is going to get bitter, then wither up, dry out and die. And guess who gets to pay for the funeral? Your dumb ass who stayed with the loser.

But He Has Potential

Here is another phrase we've heard uttered by our mothers: he's got potential. I know my mother told me that and my girlfriends' mothers have told them the same thing. We may be considering dating, getting engaged or even marrying a man, but we have reservations about fully committing to a person. First of all, no one is ever 100% sure all of the time about a relationship. So it's okay to not be certain, but it's not okay to project what you hope for in the future to become a reality in your potential mate. You shouldn't give people points for potential.

Here is the inherent problem with potential. Everyone has potential. We all have the potential to be bad and the potential to be good. We all have the potential to be a serial killer or an ambassador of goodwill, but potential is out there in the ether. People need to take steps toward their goals, real tangible steps, before they should be awarded any points for potential. Personally, I would not stake my life on potential. But if a man had said he wanted to be president someday and was in his early twenties and clerking for a senator, then I would believe that yes, he does have the potential to reach that goal. If another man had the same goal, but worked at Best Buy and he's thirty-nine, I would say he has less of a chance of meeting that goal. The difference between the Best Buy Guy and the senatorial clerk is talk. Talk is cheap, my friend, and it doesn't pay the light bill. Your man can tell you all you want to hear. He can tell you about his dreams, his goals, what kind of house he wants for you, but until he has done something real to meet those goals the talk doesn't mean a damn thing. Do not marry a big talker. Marry a doer! Real doers don't need to talk about their potential because they are living up to it. Be wary of the big dreamers with no real means of attaining the dream. Dreamers and talkers are usually too busy talking and dreaming to actually achieve anything. Stick with the guys who keep it close to the vest and get the job done!

People who are dating are not unlike politicians on the campaign trail. Politicians are trying to get votes so they'll do things they don't like to do, like pretend to enjoy doing the dishes or giving oral sex. All daters are running for office, both men and women. Like Politicians, they make campaign promises that once they are voted into office they don't keep. You need to date a man for a while and see him when he's not on his best behavior before you decide to vote him into office. Too often, we as women buy into the political double talk and cast our vote too soon for a guy who isn't who he says he is. Watch your man in action. Don't just listen to the propaganda he's feeding you. I have voted men into romantic office because they ran a good campaign, but once in office those campaign promises never came to fruition. So these men were not re-elected or in some cases they had to be impeached.

You also need to watch your man when he doesn't think you're looking. Remember how Mitt Romney got caught on camera saying that Obama had 47% of the vote locked up because that 47% were victims who just wanted to live off the government? Well that took Romney down, by exposing his true self. While dating, we must be keenly aware of off color things our dates may say, when they don't think we're listening because that may expose them for who they really are and not the guy campaigning to get into your pants or into your life.

Women are nurturers by design, which is both a flaw and an asset. It's a flaw because we will make excuses and try to help and or change a man or ourselves so that we can have the life society and our mothers told us we should have e.g.: family, children, home and career. There is nothing wrong with this life unless we try to force it upon others or ourselves when it's not meant to be. Here is how it becomes a problem. We have a picture of what our life is supposed to look like, the fantasy: engaged or with the "one" by age twenty-nine, married by thirty, have a baby by thirty-two, etc. Let's not try to live a paint by numbers sort of life because we may try to make the current boyfriend fit into the picture even though he doesn't belong. We may overlook things like a tainted job history, the fact that he looks at other women while he's with you, or his felony record because we're on a timeline. Good enough is no way to spend the rest of your life or even an afternoon. I don't want a satisfactory marriage. I don't expect every day to be spectacular, but some of us are so used to being unhappy that happy feels foreign and unfamiliar. Satisfactory is acceptable to far too many women. He's good enough and cute and I'm thirty-two, so I should just marry him. *No one has ever treated me this well.* These are things I've heard girlfriends say. Considering the fact that the last guy you dated stole money out of your bank account and illegally used your social security number--just about anyone else has treated you better than him. At least the bum on the street offered to clean your windows before he hit you up for money. So, you got an actual service out of it. Do not be too hasty with the biggest decision of your life.

Fantasy vs. Reality

Yes, we all have fantasies playing in our heads. Entire movies of what we'd like our lives to look like, our husband to look like, our house and our children. It's nice to have a fantasy, but it is not real. The reality of your life is probably sitting next to you on the couch and the fantasy is probably a lot better.

There is a medical term called phantom pain. Amputee patients often claim that they can feel the amputated limb. They truly believe it's still there until they get up to walk on their nonexistent leg and fall flat on their face. Eventually, amputee patients go through rehabilitation and learn to walk and live without the limb. They survive the loss. Often they are stronger afterwards. A marriage counselor I saw said a few words to me that literally set me free. He said that I have to stop fantasizing about what I wanted my then husband and marriage to be and face the reality of what it was. In that moment, I realized that everything I hoped and wanted our marriage and family to be was just a fantasy. The thoughts that I had about him were a confluence of my projections and not real. Once I saw my marriage for what it was, I knew it was over. There was nothing. Just a dream. A phantom marriage.

Many of us are living our lives in phantom marriages or relationships. We have this man in our lives and we have elaborate fantasies about the relationship. In our minds, the relationship is fantastic. In reality, it's broken. Our unreality allows us to continue in the relationship without facing the fact that he's cheating, he gambles, he's verbally abusive, he stinks, he's lazy, he's not supportive, or he's jealous of you. Often, we portray the fantasy relationship to the outside world so that it seems as if we have the perfect marriage or boyfriend. It isn't until we actually try to use the phantom limb that we realize it's not there and we fall flat on our face. Our husband or boyfriend isn't really who we need him to be. He isn't the man in our fantasy. He is a useless, withered up limb that needs to be cut off. Sadly, the relationship only exists in our fantasy-life. I am by no means saying that a relationship with another human being is supposed to always meet every single one of your needs. That's impossible. But when you find yourself denying what's in front of you and seeing an illusion of what you'd like your relationship to be, it's time to wake up from your trance and face reality. And by facing reality, one must have realistic expectations of a mate or partner, not super-human expectations.

I believe the truth in the Bible that says, "With God all things are possible." I also believe people can change if they acknowledge their deficit, have a willingness to change and take the limits off themselves and their future. Having said that, while in relationships of all kinds: friendships, co-workers, relatives, boyfriends, husbands et. al. the greatest disappointments I've faced in life are from expecting too much from people who have placed limits on themselves or from people who are unwilling to give more, love more and support more. What I've had to do is recognize other people's limitations in giving, loving and achieving. And that recognition has set me free. I've experienced great heartache, sleepless nights, angst, anxiety and long suffering when people did not meet my expectations. The problem has been that my expectations have exceeded what these other people have been willing or are able to give of themselves. Often I thought that because a person was my boyfriend, husband, friend or blood relative, they should treat me a certain way. They should go to the mat for me. They should fully support me, be there to listen, help, love and not in some crazy, codependent way, but in a way conducive to the relationship.

The truth is that some people are limited and set limits and boundaries for what they are willing to give, love and do. And we all have and need to have boundaries. We also need to communicate those boundaries. In my experience, when a limit or boundary is not communicated, it causes confusion, angst, and pain. It is better to tell someone you cannot do or be what that person is asking rather than avoiding his call, ignoring his email or dropping off the face of the earth. Loving and caring for another individual means respecting boundaries and limits. The truth is sometimes we expect too much of other fallible, needy human beings. I have learned to reconfigure my expectations of others and that has enabled me to let go of the dream of the way I wanted people to be and deal with the reality of who they are. It's enabled me to not deify a relationship and require it to completely fulfill me. It's enabled me to easily forgive people who have disappointed me.

I can be loved, supported and fulfilled by many different people who play unique roles in my life. And most importantly, I have a relationship with God and seek Him to fulfill me in ways no human being ever can. I think sometimes we're asking our husbands or boyfriends to be a God in our lives which is asking way too much of a mere man not to mention we're asking the wrong person. Now I no longer hold people to unrealistic expectations. I don't require things from others they cannot give. In recognizing others' limitations, it has helped me see their assets because I am not so focused on what they are not doing.

Having unrealistic expectations of a human being is like a fundraiser for a major charity choosing to ask the girl who tosses fries at McDonald's to contribute a million dollar donation for the new cancer wing at Cedars Sinai Hospital. It would be ignorant, insulting, shaming and reckless to ask so much of a person whose hourly wage is less than $10.00 dollars an hour. It would make her feel inadequate. She may want to help because it's a good cause, but she cannot give a million dollars. She simply doesn't have it to give. And if that's what the fundraiser is expecting, and nothing less, the French Fry Girl will probably feel anger towards this fundraiser. French Fry Girl may have been willing to give in her own way, but since she's been told nothing less than a million is acceptable she will probably decide not to give anything at all. So not only are the organizers of the fundraiser unable to meet their needs in terms of raising money, but they have humiliated both themselves and the McDonald's French Fry Girl and caused irreparable damage to that relationship.

So why would a woman expect a man who has self-esteem issues to be loving and kind to her when he clearly isn't that way with himself? We cannot expect a man who truly doesn't believe in himself and his abilities to be a President or CEO of a company, a breadwinner or any sort of major contributor either financially or emotionally to a relationship. We cannot expect a man who has spent most of his life in debt to suddenly spend money wisely or balance a checkbook. He is limited. Asking him to be something he's not is like demanding that a deaf person hear or that a blind person see. Once we stop trying to make a man something and someone he'll never be, we release him and we release ourselves of the unrealistic expectation. We're able to move forward with our lives. We're able to value the person for what they have to give rather than tear them down for what they are not contributing. If we choose to, we can make the relationship work in a more mutually fulfilling way. If we stay, we must recognize our partner's limitations and value their assets. If we leave, we not only recognize their limitations but ultimately our own limits in what we find acceptable and unacceptable in a relationship.

Occupy an Ambitious Girl's Couch

It's the second movement after occupy Wall Street. It's a lesser-known movement that doesn't get television coverage, but it's happening in living rooms all over this country and I imagine, the world. The occupiers come from all races, religions and socioeconomic backgrounds. My friend Ellyn is Caucasian and Ivy League educated. Her now ex-husband was a couch occupier for two years. He worked sparingly. Their family of four subsisted on her income while he indulged in expensive hobbies, watched baseball on the couch and his wife worked and took care of their children. The final straw for her in their marriage was similar to Kate's *Oprah* moment. Her husband's favorite hobby was Fantasy Baseball. One early spring day Ellyn was doing some online banking when she noticed that someone had made a three thousand dollar withdrawal from their account. That someone was her unemployed husband. When she confronted him about this enormous, unilateral withdrawal, he nonchalantly explained that it was for his Fantasy Baseball League. Ellyn, trying to remain calm, told him that is a ridiculous amount of money and that he has no right to gamble that much money, especially when he is not employed and they have a mortgage, car payments and children who eventually have to go to college, and thanks to his sub-par dental genes, will undoubtedly need braces. She told him that he could not play Fantasy Baseball this year because they could not afford it. His response was that he had to play, "I'm the commissioner of the entire Fantasy Baseball league." That was the nail in the coffin of her marriage. She realized that the potential he was not living up to would never be reached. She woke up from her fantasy of what she was hoping her husband could be to the cold, hard nightmare of what he was: a couch occupier. Perhaps Kanye West needs to update the lyrics to his song "Gold Digger" to include this un-ambitious class of men who are happy to live off their women.

TOP 5 THINGS YOU CANNOT CHANGE IN A MAN

1. You cannot give a man self-esteem or confidence
2. You cannot give a man ambition or drive.
3. You cannot teach a man how to love himself.
4. You cannot help a man get over his childhood wounds.
5. You cannot teach a man how to be a man.

Trying to give a man any of the above qualities is like trying to make a Chinese person black, or trying to get a 75-year-old person who is right-handed to become left-handed overnight. These changes need to come from within the person and not from you, girl. You can pray, hope and believe for change, but you cannot do it.

CHAPTER SIX

Our Bodies and the Bodies We Covet

Our Bodies, Ourselves is a book about women's health first published in the early 70's. It's an empowering tool for women to help us understand our sexuality and the changes our bodies go through. It's a classic feminist book. The book is an example of a tool by which to bring us together collectively as women in support of one another and educate each other about our sexuality, puberty, childbirth, menopause and everything in between. Lately, I feel as if women are pitted against each other whether it's in the plethora of reality programming that just serves a series of televised catfights (the male equivalent to this would be boxing matches where the competitors are paid a lot more money than those Housewife chicks on Bravo and given more respect as sportsmen). Or the artificial, airbrushed magazine covers of gladiator models, or celebrities shoving unattainable beauty down our throats. Kudos to my girl, Kelly Clarkson, who spoke out against her unauthorized airbrushing by *SELF* Magazine and all the other haters who criticized her body. What happened to the *Sisterhood of The Traveling Pants* type of fun, female togetherness and empowerment?

In order to combat these low dating standards and bad behavior from men, we need to come together as women and stop viewing other women as competition, but rather as compatriots.

I went to an all-girls school from first through twelfth grade and have respect, admiration and feel a sisterhood with other women that only comes from not seeing other women as competition because I didn't spend my formative years in school trying to out-do my female classmates for the attention of a male classmate. Since we didn't have any male classmates, we were in it together. I'm proud to say I'm still close with so many of my grade school classmates. Despite how our society pits women against women, I think if we all try hard enough we can form our own *Sisterhoods of the Traveling Pants-* -or purses--or Tupperware, but to get there we must value ourselves first.

The problem is we don't value our bodies ourselves. We value other women's bodies. The way the pronouns work other women need to value their bodies themselves not us. So we're doing it wrong. But that's okay because you don't know you're doing it wrong until someone shows you a way to do it better, not right, but better for you, yourself and your body.

White Men Can't Jump & They Accept It

Men compete in sports but at an early age the smaller, weaker guys understand that they will never dunk and therefore go into business, but fashion magazines taunt us into believing that even at age sixty (thanks to Suzanne Somers, who by the way has found the fountain of youth) can still look like the bombshell twenty year old cover models who really don't even look like that in person. I've spent time in the elevator with Bar Refaeli on several occasions within a six-month period and it was only because she was with Leonardo DiCaprio (and according to *US Weekly* they were a couple at the time) that I realized who she was. After the second elevator encounter, I studied her picture on the Internet and then compared her real life image the next time I saw her on the elevator. Yes, she is pretty, but in real life she looked more like a sixteen-year-old lanky teenager, than the bombshell *Sports Illustrated* cover model. Yes, she was wearing baggy clothes and a baseball hat, which probably concealed her Supermodel hotness. Yet, the moral of this story is that even the *Sports Illustrated* Cover Models don't look like that in real life. Seriously. I know we've heard models say that about themselves, but they're usually saying it when they are in full hair and make-up. Well, I'm here to tell you I've seen it with my own two eyes and cameras, make-up, a wind machine and Photoshop can work miracles--like Moses parting the Red Sea miracles.

Men understand their limits at an early age. Unless they grow two feet, they will never be LeBron James, but with makeup, hair weaves, Botox, Sensa, anorexia, hypnosis, ass implants and high heels women are hoodwinked into believing they can be Cindy Crawford. By the way, several years ago I sat in the waiting area at CAA, a talent agency, next to Cindy Crawford and studied her for a good ten minutes because she is breathtaking, like work of art breathtaking. I looked at Cindy and then I looked at myself. Then I looked at Cindy again and looked at myself and wondered am I even a woman. Staring at Cindy, who is goddess-like and super tall made me question whether or not God had designed me as some sort of intersex being not quite woman and not at all man because Cindy was just the most beautiful creature I had ever seen. I actually wondered if I was the same species as this Cindy Crawford being. She was wearing minimal make-up, but no wind machine or Photoshop. Unlike the *Sports Illustrated* model I saw in the elevator and other Hollywood so-called beauties I've seen or worked with over the years, Cindy was the exception to them all. In that waiting room, I looked at her as long as I looked at The Mona Lisa at the L'Ouvre. But,

God did make both of us descendants of Eve and we share a sisterhood and despite my envy of her everything I will not buy into this commercialization of her features and hate her and hate myself, or try to resolve the hate by buying body parts that make me look more like Cindy (I am going to buy her infomercial beauty products though). The truth is I need to accept that Cindy has gifts and I have gifts and we're not in competition and therefore we'll look out for each other in the "neighborhood wife watch" kind of way. We'll collectively expect more from men so our sister friends aren't settling and we're all expecting the best. In other words, if we all keep our prices high (expectations high) our boyfriends and husbands won't look around for a cheaper brand that they know they can use, abuse, and throw out to just buy another one that may cost even less.

Self Acceptance Begins with Ass Acceptance

So I'm no longer in competition with other women especially cover models or even real-life models. I've accepted myself. And self-acceptance begins with ass acceptance. Here is the thing about my ass. It's middle aged. I've had this butt for over four decades. I'm getting used to it. It gets bigger and smaller, but it's unique shape mostly stays intact, it's the mushiness that changes. I've had a lot of time to hate this butt,

I've waged war against it, but now I've entered a peace treaty with my rear end. I accept it for its pockets of cellulite, its round shape, the way it lacks tautness, which is nicer way of saying it's succumbing to gravity. The truth about my bum is no matter how much weight I lose, as soon as the weight comes back it lands at my back door. It's happy there. My war on my butt has been like the fight over the Gaza strip and no one wins that so I've called for peace. If I'm happy with my butt, then any man should be thrilled. I'm at the point where I can say I want my butt not Cindy Crawford's. Admittedly, there are days when I wouldn't say no to Cindy's derrière, but I have come to a place of gratitude for mine. Recently a woman behind me in spinning class pulled me aside to say, "Don't take this the wrong way, but you have a great butt," which was really nice to hear. When someone else admires what I consider to be my problem area, it gives me a new appreciation for it.

When we as women can stop being competitive with other women's body parts and happy with what God gave them and us then we can believe in ourselves enough to start focusing on our dreams and not coveting other women's butts or boyfriends. It sounds cliché, but we have to accept every last bit of ourselves before we'll attract a worthy mate. If not, we may settle for a big, fat, loser. And then we'll have to deal with his fat ass and ours.

In part I feel so strongly about not pitting woman against

woman because I've been a victim of it and have seen how the reverse works in favor of all women.

The Worst Break-up I ever had

The worst break-up I ever had was at the hands of a woman, a friend. No, this is not some story of Sapphic love. I was fifteen and dating a guy let's call him Jared because that's what that motherfella's name was. Jared was eighteen and had a car. The car was seventy-nine percent of his attractiveness. My parents didn't know I was dating an older guy with a car because I was a teenager and therefore adept at not telling them everything. Also, they practiced a sort of laissez-faire parenting, which basically means: we trust you, just don't get into any trouble and get good grades. So I could do whatever I wanted with Jared, but since I had this self-induced chastity thing going on that meant we didn't do much. I went with Jared for a few months. Things were good on my end, but I guess on his end our witty repartee was not enough to satisfy his sexual longings so he decided to dump me, but in the most cowardly way. First he picked me up from school in his Mustang and showed me an earring that he found in his car. He asked me if it was mine. I examined the earring and told him nonchalantly no, but he didn't stop there. He wondered aloud whose earring it was. I asked him if it could be his mother's and he said no. Because I never made a big deal out of the earring, he eventually dropped it. What I didn't understand was he was trying to use the earring as a red herring that he had another girl in his car. I was blithely secure in our relationship so I never thought he'd cheat on me. I never took the bait so that attempt at a break-up didn't work.

A couple weeks after the earring incident we had plans to see a concert. The Cure was coming. Yes, I was a black, suburban, teenage girl in the 80's so I listened to The Cure. Everything couldn't be all Kool and the Gang and The O'Jay's. I really wanted to see The Cure. I asked Jared if we could invite some of my girlfriends. He could drive; I couldn't, so we needed him for the ride plus I wanted him to go. He tried to get out of it. At first he said he couldn't use the Mustang so he'd have to drive the Honda, which he thought wasn't cool to drive. I was fifteen without a license or a car so I didn't care if he took us there in his snowmobile. We were going to the show. I invited two friends and Jared tried to hit on one of them. Everyone tried to hit on Mary. She's beautiful. Even I found myself lingering at her piercing blue eyes that contrasted with her curly black hair. So I wasn't really jealous of him looking at a pretty girl with whom I was somewhat enthralled with as well. Plus I knew Mary was not interested in his ass. But again I guess he was trying to initiate a break-up and these were all fine attempts, but I was this very self-possessed, strong, secure fifteen year old who was not threatened. So Jared, who clearly was not man enough to end our relationship, resorted to having a woman break up with me on his behalf. The woman he chose was my dear friend Annie Tate. Annie was tougher than Jared and almost anyone. She had an imposing body, boisterous laugh and would call people on their shit. She was bawdy, with a strong personality and wasn't afraid to fight you, mostly verbally, but she didn't seem afraid of a physical altercation either. Annie defined peer pressure. She didn't ask you to do something she didn't say, "Try this wine cooler?" She said "DRINK IT" and the it could have been grain alcohol, but you were drinking it. So when Annie told me, "Jared wants to break-up with you," I knew it was for real. That pathetic boy needed a strong woman to break up with his girlfriend. Sadly this is where the sisterhood needs to come into play. Annie should have stood up to Jared and told him to man up and dump me himself, but because Annie was such a good friend she wanted to ease the blow of the dumping and thought if it came from her I wouldn't be as hurt.

Asking Annie to break up with me was akin to the slave masters having slaves whip one another. It only fueled divisiveness. This break-up was woman against woman. But at least when Annie told me Jared was breaking up with me I knew it was final, not like wimpy, lame ass Jared's feeble attempts to breakup, which weren't really attempts. Jared was trying to goad me into breaking up with him because he wasn't man enough. He was trying to play Jedi Mind tricks on me to make me think he was cheating and start an argument over his flirting with my friend. He tried to use other women and finally literally used another woman to end our relationship. It was a punk ass, bitchy move if you ask me and another way men try to divide and conquer. I could have gotten angry with Mary for being beautiful. I could have turned on her and blamed or accused her of trying to steal my triflin' man. I could have gotten angry with the imaginary woman who left her earrings in my boyfriend's car. I could have even gotten angry with Annie. But to this day, I am friends with Mary and Annie and never heard from Jared again. Sisterhood--it works if you work it.

We should all try to be a little more like Hoda and Kathie Lee. Yes, they have wine daily, but they also have each other's back. They're supportive of one another. They are a team put together by NBC executives, but they transcended that by coming together as more than just co-hosts, but as women and friends. There seemingly is no infighting, nor jockeying for first position or more camera time. With Hoda and Kathie there is sisterhood.

The Sisterhood of the Neighborhood Watch Wives

My friend Ashley recently told me a story about a married white woman who found out her white husband was cheating on her with a black woman. Now Ashley is also black and when her married friend told her about her husband's philandering the wife seemed to put the crux of the blame on the black woman and not her husband who couldn't keep it in his pants. Suddenly this infidelity issue became a race issue and fueled the wife's excuse to be angry at all black women. Let's not lose sight of who is in the wrong here and blame our fellow woman whatever her race, religion or creed. Blaming the other woman may help you rationalize your man's cheating, but understand that is a distraction and deflection from the headline: your man's a lying, cheating, triflin' ass. I've been in relationships where I've been in an argument with my significant other about a headline issue in our relationship, but my man has attempted to deflect and distract by talking about some other little insignificant problem to bury the lead. Somehow he'd turn the tables and create World War III with our slight disagreement over the room temperature, or the one time I forgot to put gas in his car after using it. The real point with my friend Ashley's friend was her man cheated. It could have been with that blue chick Jennifer Lawrence plays in *X-MEN*, he's still a cheater regardless of the race of the woman. I know the lyrics of Kanye's song "Goldigger" hit home for many of us on different levels. And yes like Kanye sings, some men have left our brown and black asses for a white girl, but that doesn't mean we should focus our anger on the woman or her ethnicity. It's not about blue, black or white. It's about a penis that likes to wander. Put the penis and the man it belongs to on blast before you take down another woman. She may not have even known that penis was currently under contract with another owner.

Cheating is a well-honed skill. It's not "Amateur Night at the Apollo" for most of these guys. They are well schooled in the art of philandering and that's how they hook us. Men, who I didn't know were married have hit me on. I've been intimate with men and then found out later they had live-in girlfriends. Don't be so quick to blame the one he cheated with because she may have been a victim in the whole matter too.

While working as an assistant on a short-lived NBC sitcom in the '90's, there was a pretty blonde, big boobed girl working there as a production assistant. The 98% male writing staff ogled her, debated about whether her boobs were real or not, chatted her up, asked for her production assistance in non-production matters and basically sexually harassed her mostly behind her back, but sometimes to her front, while gawking at her breasts. The female line producer of the show noticed all of the attention this young girl was getting from the mostly married writing staff and she did not like it. As the male attention waxed onto this production assistant, her job security waned. At first the female producer demoted her to set P.A. as a means to keep her away from the male writing staff.

Then she was demoted again to the set phone P.A. Before cell phones and email, there was a phone on the stage that didn't ring, but lit-up to alert one of a call. It didn't ring so as not to disrupt filming. The blonde, booby, P.A. got demoted to the position of sitting by that phone and watching for the light to illuminate so that she could answer. The thing is the phone was positioned right at the door of the stage so when all the male writers had to enter the stage, she was the first person they encountered and since she had been taken away from them, they spent inordinate amounts of time by the phone chatting her up and staring at her boobs. Finally the female producer, as a means of looking out for the terrified wives of the writers, fired the blonde, booby girl, which I thought was a pretty shitty move. Essentially she was punished for being hot. In that way the sisterhood of the neighborhood wives attacked their own. Unacceptable. The enemy is not the pretty young girl. It's the husbands with wandering eyes and penises.

The neighborhood watch wives actually helped me get employment once. I was being considered for a position as an assistant to a Hollywood producer. His former assistant was leaving and she happened to be a married woman. Her married boss had a penchant for blondes. She was not a blonde, nor was I. Being a black woman I never had a shot at being a natural blonde and this job was way before Mary J. Blige and Beyoncé, the black women's blonde haired trailblazers. I was the former assistant's first choice for the position and I got the job. This was a different kind of affirmative action hire. I was hired to affirm that my new boss, a.k.a. the husband who liked blondes, wouldn't be getting any on the job action. The neighborhood wife watch brigade is a powerful group.

Here are a couple of examples of how the Sisterhood of the Neighborhood Watch Wives worked for the greater good and called errant husbands and boyfriends out on their actions. Both of them happened to me.

In my twenties, I attended a wedding in my hometown of Cleveland. I was living in Los Angeles at the time. I met a guy at the wedding and it was one of those meet-cute situations that romantic comedies are written about. The guy, let's call him Joe, was also a wedding guest. He was a few years my senior. We chatted, danced and drank. At the end of the night my girlfriends were all a flutter with excitement that I met someone. I was too. He mentioned he was summering in the Vineyard and I had plans to visit the Vineyard that summer. He asked me for my number and email. Once I got back to L.A. we started emailing, which progressed into phone calls, though he often called me at odd times. His calls usually came around 11p.m. Pacific Time, which was 2 a.m. Eastern Time. Also, he started to get vague about his Vineyard plans and that's when my radar went up. Because he was from my hometown and connected with a friend's older brother, I called my girlfriend to get the 411 on this guy. She told me she thought he had a girlfriend, but wasn't sure, but her mother would be able to really give us the deets on his romantic life and everything else. Cleveland, though a metropolis, is still a very small town. One night my girlfriend conferenced in her mother. I told her mother the situation and how Joe was calling me at odd hours and had once seemed excited to meet me in the Vineyard, but was now seeming lukewarm. She told me that Joe had a live-in girlfriend and she probably wasn't at the wedding because she was a doctor and she was on-call. That's right. Joe was busted.

The next time Joe phoned me at two in the morning I called that brotha on his shit. "Why are you calling me in the middle of the night? Is your girlfriend asleep or at the hospital saving lives?" I said, putting him on blast. He stuttered, then stammered. "Um-hmm. Well ah-ah-ah." Yeah, I thought so. Joe apologized. I'm not sure whether he was apologizing for getting caught or for his behavior. I don't know if his girlfriend ever caught him, but I do know they eventually broke up.

Taking full account of my history with men who have tiptoed across the cheating line and my girlfriend's histories I've come up with a theory. A majority of married or involved men have to dip their toe into the pool to see if the cheating waters are warm enough for them to dive in. So many of them do it. Even the ones who you'd never think would dare seem to have this innate need to try. Then there are the ones who may not outright proposition you to have a liaison, but they are boldly flirtatious with single women and only when their wives are not around. I'm sure you've had that handsy, flirty, male co-worker who can't seem to get enough of you 9 to 5, but come time for the company barbecue or Christmas party he attends with his wife, he acts like you're a total stranger. I have so much more respect for the men of integrity who I've encountered, befriended and worked alongside who hold their vows sacred and do not feel the need to test the cheating waters at all.

Perhaps my radar sounded an alarm so early about Joe because I had experienced something similar, early in my twenties. One of my first jobs out of college was working for ABC network. Every year we'd attend the networks fall launch party. This was a party where network stars of old and new series along with the series creators and network employees would imbibe, eat and kick off the fall season. This was in the 90's and one of the hit shows on ABC at the time was *NYPD BLUE*. At the party I spoke to a young Claire Danes whose series *My So Called Life* was about to premiere. Later in the night, I moved on to chat with actors from a new and short-lived show called *Murder One*. Steven Bochco, who also produced *NYPD Blue*, produced *Murder One*.

While hanging out with the *Murder One* folks, I was introduced to an actor, who appeared on *NYPD Blue*. We chatted, drank and even danced a little (I apologize that my mating pattern in all my encounters with men is the same: chatting, alcohol and dancing. In the future I'll try to change it up some). We separated during the party, mingling with others, and then reconnected later. Things were flirtatious and though he was older than me, I was a little attracted, but my attraction wasn't just sexual. I knew at that time I wanted to be a writer and I had come from an acting background so I felt a kinship with these actors because I'm an artist too. My hope was not to just make a personal connection, but also a professional one, but at twenty-four, I was naïve enough to believe I could achieve both or just the professional part. Anyway, the party was waning and I told the nameless *NYPD Blue* actor that I was going to leave. We hugged and kissed goodbye on the cheek, then he offered to walk me out. As we made our way up the stairs, he was very chivalrous, opening the door and guiding me up the stairs by lightly resting his hand on my lower back. I was twenty-four, it seemed chivalrous at the time, now I know he was making his big move. He told me he'd like to see me again. Maybe I could come to the set, or we could get together? As we walked up the stairs, chatting, laughing, clearly engaged, we passed by some of his fellow cast mates including the wife of one of the actors on the show. As he said hello, he turned his back to me. Not at all chivalrous and he didn't introduce me. However the boisterous and bold wife of one of the cast mates did acknowledge me by introducing herself and asking who I was. My *NYPD Blue* actor/friend seemed caught so caught that he explained to the wife that, "Hey, this isn't what it looks like. Nothing is going on here." And the good wife said quite loudly, "I know nothing is going on because your wife would kill you!" Right then and there the *NYPD Blue* actor got cold busted by a neighborhood watch wife. I was grateful for her blunt, bold and loud statement. She saw something and she said something (which our government tells us to do when suspicious of terror and also a philandering husband) and prevented me from having a dalliance with a married man. In that moment, I was thankful for the sorority of wives that held all husbands to a high standard. The *NYPD Blue* actor walked me out of the Beverly Hills Hotel where we were met with paparazzi. I made sure to step away from him so that we weren't photographed together. When he asked me why, I told him I didn't need for my mother to see me in *US Magazine* photographed with a married man. Thankfully, I never heard from the Detective, but I continued to watch *NYPD Blue*.

Winners Never Cheat In Romance

I have friends who have had relationships with married men. Rationalizations and excuses are made and they find themselves entangled in an affair. Sometimes the marriages are really over, but just not legally, which is why excuses and rationalizations are needed. The bottom line is a marriage is a covenant, which means it's an enormous promise. It's bigger than the promise that you made to the bank that you're going to pay your credit card bill. Bloomingdales is not going to hunt you down for taking their man. Marriage is a biblical promise where the actual bible is usually involved or at least invoked. Marriage came from the Bible. So it's a sacred, big deal, lalapalooza, promise. Whether you're in this kind of situation or know someone who is the bottom line is that extra-marital affairs are destructive, messy and just plain icky. Every extra-marital situation I've ever heard about has an "ick" factor. I once heard a story that serves as the best analogy for cheating that describes the "ick" in a tangible way.

A few years ago a friend of mine was shopping at a posh West Hollywood boutique. She saw a pair of leather pants she was dying to have. The salesgirl retrieved the pants from the window and mentioned in hushed tones that a famous award-winning actress had just tried these pants on too. My friend went into the changing room and began to undress with eager anticipation. As she pulled on the leather pants she noticed something disgusting in the crotch: a snail trail. Yes, the previous award-winning actress had left vaginal secretions in the pants. Ick! And ladies, that's what it is like when you date a married man. You are wearing some other woman's marked pants. Those leather pants like the married man are not the only pair of leather pants in the universe. Yes, they may be on sale, or look great on you, but some other woman has marked those pants like a dog marks his territory. Those are not your pants. He is not your man. If you truly believe there will never be another pair of leather pants out there for you and you buy them, I don't care how much you have them cleaned, you'll always know those are really another woman's pants. If you compromise your beliefs and decide to keep those pants, like the snail trail left behind, your decision will ultimately make you sick.

Keep Your Boyfriends Close and Your Girlfriends Closer

Back in 1999 when I got engaged, the prevalent doctrine in pop culture regarding marriage and dating was the book *The Rules*. *The Rules*, the notion of the one--every article in every woman's magazine with tips on how to get him to notice you, engagement chicken and all those J Lo wedding, romantic comedies made it seem like getting a man to wed you was some kind of game and if you played by the litany of rules suggested by books, magazines and movies after a roasted chicken dinner, you should get a ring. And the ring was the ultimate goal. Now

I never read *Lord of the Rings* because after I read *The Hobbit*, I was kind of done with J.R.R. Tolkien, but the fellowship of the ring has become the dialogue for single women. In the late 90's, we came together as groups to watch *Ally McBeal* lament over love and then a few years later we collectively started to watch *The Bachelor*. We waited with bated breath at that moment the Bachelor would choose his bride and present her with the coveted ring. Before the late, great, Joan Rivers was ousted from red carpets she would always advise young women who were accompanied by boyfriends to, "Get a ring, honey." On the now defunct Dr. Laura Schleshinger show she would always ask female callers who said they were engaged if they had a ring and a date because that signified a real engagement. I prayed with other single female friends that God would bring us husbands. Other friends who got engaged always had elaborate engagement stories that involved Hawaii and sometimes helicopters, or hiding the ring in food. This became part of the game with the ultimate prize being the ring and then the wedding. But somewhere along this thrilling, romantic ride the actual marriage got lost. Women's magazines don't really talk much about maintaining your marriage. I have yet to read the article entitled: "I'm sick of my husband today and he bought an iPad, which means now I can't buy those shoes that I wanted. So I'm going to say something mean to him and I may withhold sex." Those articles aren't as sexy, I suppose, but neither is marriage.

Anyway, I fell into that romanticized version of engagement and marriage and started playing the game to win and guess what, I did win! Sort of...I wanted to get invited into married people's land and have couple friends and parties. It was like an exclusive club I had heard about my entire life, but could never be a part of until now. My ring was my invitation. And even before I got my ring other couple friends were recruiting me. And this was hardcore recruiting as if I were the top high school football player and colleges and coaches were dying to get me to sign with their university. The female halves of my then boyfriend's couple friends were like used car salesmen or Jehovah's witnesses. Before I got engaged, my boyfriend asked me to move in with him. I was on the fence about moving in because I knew that I wanted to be married and I had made a decision that the only way I'd live with a man was if we were engaged first. While I was mulling over my moving in together decision, I think my then boyfriend had lamented about my reluctance to some of his couple friends and the female partners took it upon themselves to do some lobbying. This was hardcore lobbying like the pharmaceutical lobbyists, who are truly gifted people because they've persuaded our government to approve of drugs that have side effects like cancer and loss of bladder and bowel control and the growth of female breasts and lactation in young boys. The pharmaceutical companies should recruit these chicks as their lobbyists. Anyway, I started getting calls from one woman in particular about the merits of moving in with my boyfriend and that he probably wouldn't be my boyfriend for long once we moved in together. She told me that she didn't really have intentions to live with her boyfriend before they got engaged, but she did and now she had the coveted ring and a date. Other women would pull me aside at parties not to ask me if we were moving in together, but when we were moving in together. And once I got engaged, these living in sin lobbyists became my new friends, who offered to host my showers and go wedding dress shopping and guide me on my bridal journey. My other single friends were around, but these engaged and married women seemed to have the expertise and since I was going to become a member of their club, I hitched my wagon to their stars.

    I did move in with my boyfriend and four months later I got my ring. I boasted about my engagement especially to people I hadn't seen in a long time. Saying I was engaged made it sound like I had achieved something and since I wasn't where I wanted to be in my career, this was my big feat. Plus, after all, I had played the game and won the prize. In some cases, I flaunted that ring around like Ryan Lochte and his gold medals. I shoved it in peoples' faces as if I'd achieved something of envy when really the exclusive club I was part of was no better than a Costco membership.

Before I had ever been to Costco I remember hearing people discuss it and the ultimate deals and buys one could get there if you had a membership. Costco seemed elusive to me and had a shroud of mystique, kind of like marriage. I also thought Costco was more of a place for married people and families so as a single girl with no need to buy in bulk I didn't feel eligible for a Costco membership. When the veil is lifted, Costco is just a warehouse full of cheap crap in big containers with crowds and long lines, few parking spaces and screaming children. And by the time you leave, you've spent more than you wanted and bought things you don't need, argued with loved ones, strangers, and lost time you can never get back again, but you got bargains and that's the American way. The experience of Costco: the lines, the screaming, demand to show your membership I.D. is similar to what I imagine took place on Ellis Island. People left both places having undergone a quintessentially harrowing American experience and thankful that they made it through the journey alive. And upon leaving Costco you can stop at their food counter and buy an All-American chilidog at a discount price and TUMS in bulk. Once the shroud of marriage is unveiled it's kinda like Costco.

With my engagement ring, I had gained entrance into a club I called: Married People's Land. Suddenly I'd get invited as a couple to a wedding, which meant I didn't have to sit at the singles table in back anymore and feel bad about myself and then be forced to engage in hand-to-hand combat with other women over the bridal bouquet. I could go on dates with other couple friends, who normally wouldn't hang out with single old me on a Saturday night. We were invited to spend holidays with other couples and their families because now we were legit. I could stay home on New Year's Eve with my husband and not feel like a loser because I wasn't alone and I had someone to kiss. I didn't completely abandon my single girlfriends. I invited them to overspend on hideous mauve colored bridesmaid dresses and hold up my wedding gown when I peed.

Previous to my engagement, I was not that type of girl to dump her friends when she got a man. I had been on the dumpee side of that equation and it was a lonely place. Coming from an all-girls school background, we weren't too quick to dump our friends for guys. Our girl power bonds were very strong. I'd always maintained my single girlfriend relationships whenever I began dating someone, but when I got engaged and then married I entered into a new land and that didn't leave much room for my girls, but thankfully some of them didn't abandon me.

Here's the thing: men will come and go, your girls will be around forever. You may even get married, but outlive your husband, so make sure you maintain your relationships with your female friends. Even if your man is around, he does not want to hear girl talk. And your husband cannot be your everything. If you divorce or separate, your married people's land card will be revoked immediately and without notice. If you haven't maintained your relationships with your single girlfriends, your banishment from married peoples land will be even more humbling because now you'll be in lonely divorced ladies' land which can be filled with alcohol, regret, tears and gnashing of teeth. The alcohol, tears and regret don't last forever. Some couple friends will surround you the days, weeks and perhaps a month and a half following your divorce. They'll invite you over for dinner. They may even invite you to a movie or to be their third wheel at a party. But like death the sitting shiva for your marriage won't last long and your married couple friends' invitations will cease and desist until you find another man. Maybe occasionally the wife will invite you to lunch, but you'll no longer be welcome to the 4th of July, or Easter brunch as a single gal. You are now bait for their husbands. And remember I said husbands love to dip their toe in the cheating waters? Since many women actually lose weight during their divorce, those married bitches want you as far away from their husbands as possible. Trust me. I have been there. I was a size four during my divorce and had to buy new skinny jeans because my old skinny jeans were too big. My divorce was the best diet ever and the easiest. I ate stress and anger for breakfast, sorrow for lunch and a petit Syrah for dinner and dessert. So trust me married women don't want divorced women wearing bikinis at their 4th of July cook out especially when they are wearing a bathing suit with a skirt and a cover-up.

Single, divorced women are like girls who get kicked out of their sorority so unless you've kept some friends outside of the married sisterhood, it will be a lonely couple of semesters for you. So when you meet a man do not make your girls file a missing persons report. You can keep your boyfriend close, but always keep your girlfriends closer.

CHAPTER SEVEN

Post Traumatic Dating Disorder Recovery Plan

Some of us have scars from PTDD, Post Traumatic Dating Disorder. We've had terrible, debilitating, dating experiences that have made us question everything, even God. Some of these experiences are so unnerving that we exhibit signs of PTDD with new men who haven't even treated us poorly. We cannot bring old baggage into a new relationship. Would you bring the bikini and sundress you packed for a trip to Hawaii on your ski vacation in Aspen? Or how about the reverse? If you bring your skis, boots, North Face parka and all the other ski paraphernalia to a Hawaiian vacation, then all you're doing is lugging that stuff around. Your ski baggage encumbers you. It's weighing you down. You're so bothered by it that you cannot stop and enjoy the present moment of your Hawaiian vacation because you're concentrating on your ski crap. When we bring past hurts and old wounds into our new relationships we're not allowing ourselves to truly experience the new because we're stuck in the old. Sometimes space and time are the only things that will enable you to truly empty your old bags before going on a new trip.

My dear friend Janet was married for twelve years to a negative, miserly, hopeless man. After her divorce she started dating a new man. Janet's friends invited her and her new boyfriend on a mini vacation, but Janet turned down the offer without even checking with her boyfriend. She turned down the offer because she presumed her new boyfriend wouldn't want to spend the money on the trip because they had just come from a vacation. One night at dinner with Janet, her friends and her boyfriend, the friends mentioned their disappointment that they had declined the offer for the mini vacation. Janet's boyfriend said this was the first he had heard about it. Janet explained she assumed he wouldn't want to spend the money. Her boyfriend retorted that he didn't have a problem with the money and he'd love to go. Janet realized that she was putting her ex-husband's negative, miserly attributes onto her new boyfriend. Her ex-husband would have been angry and annoyed that Janet even dared to ask if they could go on the mini vacation after just returning from another vacation. Janet brought the trauma that she faced in her marriage to her relationship with her boyfriend. She brought her skis to the beach.

Hopefully, you all have treated old relationship wounds and learned your lesson from the former man and have not chosen the same type of guy again. If you haven't learned your lesson, you will keep choosing the same guy until you do.

When dating we have to lose our old baggage just like the airlines lose luggage every day. Leave it on the tarmac, girl. Adopt a new attitude for dating. Yes, perhaps it's been a while since you've had any male attention, at least attention from someone you're interested in. And maybe it's been even longer since someone has taken you out on a proper date and kissed you goodnight. Perhaps you're cynical. You have doubt and fear. That's understandable, but also know that you may be exuding your doubt and fear and that's not attractive. The thing is whatever awful break-up, divorce or bad dating experience left you with some form of PTDD, you have survived it. If you're reading this book, you are a SURVIVOR. You may be in the early stages of survival, or three years post break-up. The point is it didn't kill you. So you're strong because you're here and you made it through, which means that bad relationship is in the rearview mirror and you need to look ahead. Adopt a new attitude in dating. Have hope. Whenever I'm going through something difficult and my problems are consuming, hope seems so far away, but it is the belief in something better that gets me through. Kelly's song "Stronger" is great and empowering. There is also a scripture that illuminates my point. Romans 5:3-5 -- "Not only so, but we also rejoice in our sufferings, because we know that suffering produces perseverance; perseverance, character; and character, hope. And hope does not disappoint us, because God has poured out his love into our hearts by the Holy Spirit, who he has given us."

Why "Call Me Maybe" Is the Right Attitude in Dating

While "maybe" is not an attitude of great hope, it's also not an attitude of doom and gloom. "Maybe" allows for the possibility. I believe that Carly Rae Jepsen's song is the attitude that women should have in dating. At least it's the perspective that I think will get you a call and I don't mean maybe. I think it guarantees a call because the attitude of maybe is aloof, ambivalent or better yet nonchalant. "Call Me Maybe" signifies that you have a lot going on and if he wants to call that's okay and if he doesn't call you will live to see another day. You'll actually do more than live, more than survive--you will thrive because his call does not make or break your life. You're not losing sleep over the call. You're not wasting hours analyzing the call or non-call or text with your girlfriends. You're not even reading self-help books about it because you couldn't care less. Often women suffering from PTDD exhibit signs of desperation. So when a man throws a woman a crumb she gobbles it down like it's the last supper. Well he is not the last guy on earth so don't act like it. There will be another man passing through in a few minutes just like the number 14 cross-town bus. Maybe says this is not the last man on earth. "Maybe" is the opposite of desperate.

Life would be so much better if we were able to manage and re-calibrate our expectations for everything. "Maybe" allows us to not expect a promise of yes or an outcome of no. "Maybe" says I'm not going to call him. "Maybe" leaves it up to fate. "Maybe" is empowering. We all know the lyrics to the song. Let's now put it into action. Think about how many of us have gone on to live happy, profitable, fulfilling lives without receiving a call from some guy. "Maybe" is never the end of the world or the end of your dating career.

Dating and Detective Work

Trust is key to any relationship, but when you don't have trust thank God for the Internet. In the cases where I had men who were being less than honest with me, I was lucky enough that someone else's wife and my friend's mom stepped in to tell me the truth about those men. I've had other friends who haven't been so lucky. Read Judy's story below and find out.

Beware of an Asshole in Dreamboat's Clothing

My friend Judy met a guy in bible study, a seemingly safe place to meet a man. They attended the study for some time before Ben finally asked Judy out on a date. They went out a few times and Judy was completely drawn to this man, but in an almost unhealthy way. On one of their first dates Ben said something strange to Judy. He said he had to go away for a bit and would be out of touch. When Judy asked why, he explained that he would be in Washington State visiting a friend who was in the FBI or part of the witness protection program. Judy wasn't quite sure which one it was. When she relayed the story back to me and another girlfriend, she kind of glossed over that last bit of information to which we said, "Hold up, rewind and go back to the part where the brotha said he was in the FBI or witness protection." She corrected us. "He's not in the FBI or witness protection program," she said pleading his triflin' defense, "At least I don't think he is," she added. All she knew was that he somewhat regularly attended this open to the public bible study. So he allegedly loved Jesus. She also knew he was cute and had a good job.

This criterion alone is more than enough for many women to decide to spend the rest of their lives with a guy, but Judy knew there was something off about his weird FBI witness protection comment. She asked us if she should pursue this guy because she really liked him. Our question to her was: do you like him more than you like being alive because if he is in the witness protection program then any association with him could put your life in jeopardy. She of course said no, but I could tell she was thinking: he's cute, employed and a Christian. My thought was if she was going to take a chance with him she better hope God can protect her because people held in federal protection die all the time. At least they do in the movies. Anyway, Judy along with our coercion, which included re-naming Ben to Witness Protection, decided that she shouldn't pursue this guy and perhaps this was a sign. As it turned out Ben was true to his word and was out of touch with Judy.

After a nearly nine-month absence, Ben started showing up to bible study again. By this point Judy had hardened to him. She even referred to him as Witness Protection. She rebuffed his advances, but true to the law of attraction, that just peaked his interest. Others in her bible study who knew Ben encouraged her to give him a chance. Judy knew that Ben did some mentoring of youth and at the time Judy knew some students who needed mentoring by a successful businessman like Ben. So in the name of helping the children, Judy acquiesced and met Ben for coffee to discuss mentoring. It became clear that the coffee meeting was a date and Judy and Ben began dating for a year, but it was a tumultuous period of time and Judy battled her gut instincts that were telling her Ben wasn't being authentic. We wondered if he was gay. There was something that wasn't right, but she couldn't put her finger on it.

Ben traveled a lot for business, which meant they spent a lot of time apart (when a man travels a lot for business that could be code for he has a wife, a girlfriend or even another dude on the side). Judy tried to attribute the unsettling feeling she had about Ben to his excessive travel. He was telling her everything she wanted to hear. He was affectionate, asked to date her exclusively, lavished her with gifts, attended church together and spoke of marriage. Ben was running a good campaign, but something still didn't sit right with Judy. And there was turmoil in the relationship especially when Ben couldn't spend Thanksgiving with Judy or his schedule got so busy that he didn't have time for her, but would make time to watch football with his boys. When Judy questioned some of his behavior, he always turned it upon her. What ensued was nothing short of psychological warfare. Despite the fact that Ben wanted to be with Judy, he couldn't always accommodate her and when Judy tried to talk rationally about her feelings, Ben turned it around so that he made Judy seem too needy, demanding and suffocating, even though at most he saw Judy once per week. Just as soon as Judy had enough of Ben's mercurial behavior and disconnectedness and had resolved to end things, she'd suddenly change her mind about breaking up with him. Some outside force changed her mind, but that nagging feeling in her gut was still there lingering and hovering over their relationship like a dark, cumulous storm cloud that was ready to blow.

Things in Ben's life began to take a turn for the worse. He became mysterious with Judy just like he did in the beginning with the FBI/ witness protection reference. Finally, after a week of putting Judy off, he finally told her the truth all about all his lies. Ben had been acting so mysterious because he had impregnated his ex-girlfriend and he just had her get a paternity test that proved that the baby was his. He knew this would be the end of his relationship with Judy, but somehow made this more about himself and his loss, not even considering how devastating this betrayal was to Judy.

Judy never saw him again, but even Ben's confession didn't sit well with her. First of all, he said he only had sex with his ex-girlfriend once, which as women we know that's a lie. That's the lie men tell their wives, girlfriends and themselves to weaken the blow of infidelity. It's also a condescending lie because it basically communicates that, "I think so little of you that I'm going to cheat, but then I'm going to lie about the amount of cheating and assume you're going to believe that lie." We're not stupid. One is already a liar if one is a cheater so why should we, as women, believe any of the shit that comes out of a cheating, liar's mouth after the first lie is exposed. Judy wanted the truth and she deserved it. So by divine intervention, also known as Facebook, she was able to uncover the truth about Ben. Judy knew the name of Ben's ex-girlfriend because they had talked about her. So Judy did some Facebook reconnaissance. She was still Facebook friends with her lying, cheating, ex Ben and his mother. Older people aren't as adept at FB so they don't know how to use all the privacy settings, which enables a person who is snooping to get all up in their business. The baby momma/Ben's ex-girlfriend was also friends with Ben's mother. So Judy was able to infiltrate her account and her families' accounts to learn Ben was leading a double life. Judy noticed pictures and dates from pictures and parties that Ben attended. These were dates that he told Judy he was out of town on business. Members of his baby momma's family tagged Ben in many of these pictures. In fact, from all the Facebook pictures she could track Ben's whereabouts on all the major holidays of the last year and his birthday. These were all dates Ben said he had to go out of town to be with his immediate family, or a friend who needed him or business. While in the relationship with Ben, Judy was beginning to think that he had an unusual attachment to his mother, but the truth was the other woman in his life was his old girlfriend. And what the Facebook pictures revealed is that she wasn't really his old girlfriend because they never broke up. The pictures depicted their relationship history and his duplicity. He looked genuinely happy at every family and holiday event. The Facebook pictures also revealed that Ben had lied about her pregnancy. She was clearly further along than he had confessed. Judy even learned from Facebook that the two moved in together shortly before Ben confessed his deceit to Judy. This man had weaved an intricate web of lies and deceit on par with the FBI. If his powers were used for good, who knows what he could have achieved. Instead the dark cloud that hovered over their relationship burst open like a toxic spill. Facebook is a friend to some, but a foe to others. The lesson here is if you're leading a double life be careful who is posting and tagging you in Facebook pictures. And the overarching lesson is trusting your gut. It never lies. Even if you don't know what it's saying, or if all it's saying is "something is rotten in Denmark" or downtown Philly, or wherever you reside, listen and obey your gut, girls.

As single women, we have to resort to extreme measures to protect ourselves in dating. To guard oneself against situations like Judy's, Facebook may not be enough. There are other Internet services you can use to do thorough background checks on potential nannies or employees. I advise you put your man's name and social security number in those systems and get a thorough background check (Beyond the Dickfax) before you let him into your home, your life and your panties.

CHAPTER EIGHT
Men and Irritable Bowel Syndrome

It seems as if all the commercials and print ads for products that cure irregularity issues are marketed toward women. Those new ads for laxatives that don't cause bloating and the yogurt that promises to regulate your digestion in two weeks all have women talking about their digestive issues. I contend that seemingly more women than men are suffering from I.B.S. and other digestive problems because we aren't listening to our guts, These problems can be caused by stress. Our guts are trying to tell us something like: get out of the bad relationship, lose the loser man in your life, or he is cheating. Trust your gut. Our digestive problems are indications that our lives are not in order. Our guts may be dysfunctional because we're in dysfunctional relationships.

One of the things that compelled me to write this book was the fact that the many women I talked to or heard stories about were smart women. Not just college graduates but Ivy League college graduates with master's degrees, law degrees and common sense, but every one of them told the same story in hindsight about their triflin' husbands or ex-boyfriends. They did not trust their instincts. In fact, they denied their instincts. One girlfriend knew that her husband was cheating. She could feel it, but he denied it. She denied her gut that was telling her the truth. Another friend knew her boyfriend would eventually disappear on her, but she denied that feeling and guess what he did disappear. My best friend denied her gut that told her while I was engaged that my then fiancé was not right for me, but she said nothing. I got married and divorced. In *The Gift of Fear* Gavin DeBecker writes that fear truly is a gift. In Elaine Aron's book, *The Highly Sensitive Person,* she describes how intuitive and sensitive people in the past were able to warn their tribes against danger, whether it was the enemy, animal predators, or bad weather. Those people were revered for their intuitive gift. Why do we as women deny ours especially when it comes to men? We want to believe the best about people. We want so much for our relationships to work out, but at the cost of denying ourselves on so many levels. Trust your gut when it comes to a man and if it's telling you something is off, it probably is. When you stop trusting yourself, you are killing off a little part of you. Denying who you are robs your soul and your spirit. Don't rationalize away the truth your gut is telling you.

Can We Be Allergic to Men

Wouldn't life be that much easier if we had some sort of crazy immune response to bad men like we break out into hives whenever a cheater, liar, or loser approaches us? Sometimes I think we just get used to the bad guys and build up immunity to them.

My entire life I've suffered with debilitating allergies. I'm allergic to benign things like grass, trees, flowers, dogs, cats, dust mites and penicillin. I've sneezed, sniffled, snorted, coughed, wheezed, suffered from a closed throat and hives, swelled up and endured red, watery, itchy eyes throughout my entire life. I've been on every known allergy medicine for the last thirty plus years. I endured immunization allergy shots since childhood, then allergy immunization drops. I even had sinus surgery, but I still suffer from allergies. And the thing about the suffering is that after thirty years of sneezing, and wheezing you get used to it. You get used to the misery.

On a recent check-up my doctor looked into my nose and exclaimed that it was incredibly inflamed and I must really be suffering from allergies. She asked me if I wanted her to prescribe a dose of steroids because I was probably miserable. The truth was I wasn't miserable. I had been much worse and though the inside of my nose indicated acute allergies and misery, my tolerance for allergic suffering is so high that I was coping. Unfortunately, abuse in bad relationships becomes so routine that as women we develop a high tolerance to the abuse, the pain, the neglect and misery that is part and parcel to being in a bad relationship. We have grown so accustomed to the pain that we don't even feel it anymore or notice it until someone points it out and dares to say, you could be living a better life. You could be in a happy, edifying, uplifting, loving relationship. Don't become accustomed to misery in any form.

What's too bad about my intense allergic reactions is that it doesn't work on men who are no good for me. I don't suddenly break out into hives, or wheeze when a loser guy who will eventually treat me bad approaches. Although, my allergies did inadvertently help me out of a bad relationship. In my twenties, I dated a man who had a dog and dog hair all over his house. I ended up suffering during that relationship and not just from his sometimes-questionable behavior, but also from his dog. When I went to see my allergy/asthma doctor to see if there was anything he could prescribe to help me deal with my asthma and allergies due to my boyfriend's dog, his prescription was to break up with the guy. It was the best medical advice I ever received because the guy was not right for me and not just because of his dog.

I once had a boyfriend who didn't believe I was allergic to dogs. This should have been a red flag in our relationship that this mofo couldn't and wouldn't take my word for it. It should have made me mad, which it did, but not mad enough to break up with him. Sadly, at that time, I valued being in a relationship with him more than I valued myself. The boyfriend knew I didn't like dogs and he thought I used allergies as an excuse to not be around dogs. He wanted me to change to appease him. Women change a lot of things for men: our breasts, our hair, our butts, but this was something I could not change.

Since my dog-loving boyfriend didn't believe me or value me guess what he did next? Friends of his just had a new baby and he wanted to visit them. Their child was too young to take out in public. They invited us to come visit at their house, but they had a dog. I warned my then boyfriend that I was very allergic to dogs and maybe there was some sort of compromise because I didn't think I would be able to spend much time in their house. He had no empathy for me and basically asked me to suck it up and take my allergy medicine so we could go to their house, which I did. When we arrived, they assured me that they put the dog in the back of the house so he wouldn't bother me. Here's the thing about people who say they put the dog in the back of the house so it won't bother your allergies: that shit doesn't work. Because guess what, the dog lives in the house and his dog hair is all over everything. So unless you put your dog away and then give your entire house a Silkwood-like scrub down erasing all traces of dog, I can still have a reaction to the animal even though you've put him in the back room of your house. And that's exactly what happened at my boyfriend's friends' home. By the time we left the visit, I was sneezing, wheezing, hoarse, coughing and rubbing my red eyes. My then boyfriend had the audacity to say, "Wow, I guess you're really allergic to dogs." No shit asshole. I dated that guy way too long.

I was often made to feel bad, or different in a negative way, about my allergies. My allergies have been alienating and embarrassing. I was also made to feel as if somehow it was my fault, but like Lady Gaga says "I was born this way" so I'm enough, allergies and all. If someone cannot accept that, then eff them. I was trying to please my boyfriend by enduring an evening with a dog rather than being true to myself and protecting myself. In the other case, I was trying to be accommodating with the boyfriend who had the dog rather than thinking about my health first. As women, we should never compromise our health, our lives, our beliefs and our truth over any person and especially over a man. Any man who asks you to compromise your health is not a man who truly cares about you.

Let Your Light Shine

I've been in relationships and I've had friends in relationships in which we've had to dim our lights to accommodate our respective partners. Let me tell you about my friend Shelly. Shelly had a great sense of humor and always regaled us with witty stories until she met John. John was a nice enough guy, but was kind of milk toast bland. Unfortunately, John was under the impression that he was witty and charming. When Shelly and John started going out, I noticed that Shelly stopped telling her witty stories to allow John to tell his non-witty ones. John's stories and jokes were kind of like the ones a grandfather tells that aren't funny, but you laugh anyway, because he's old and may die soon and leave you money. Shelly stopped being Shelly. She seemed to lose her sense of humor. Her sister and I noticed this, but didn't know what to do. As her relationship progressed with John, her light seemed to grow more dim. She was once someone who would light up a room with her wit, but now she was practically mute and let John steal her spotlight.

If you become a lesser version of yourself for a man, he's not the man for you. Years later Shelly divorced John and found her sense of humor again. Sacrifices that diminish and change who you are aren't worth it. Even the Bible says to let your light shine.

My dear friend Abby has a great personality: charming, witty, beautiful--the full package. She also exudes confidence and a strong sense of herself. She met a guy, Jake, who was very nice and handsome, but who didn't have very much personality. When Abby comes into a room, you always know it. When Jake comes into a room, you would probably miss it. Jake and Abby got married and he struggled with depression throughout the marriage. He never wanted to go anywhere or do anything. He took up residence on the couch. Abby stayed at home with him and sat on the couch next to him for years until she had a light-bulb moment. I knew Abby wasn't happy and I asked her what was going on. She said to me that there was a problem in her marriage and she felt as if she had dimmed her light for this man. She later divorced him and let her light shine again.

You Have To Feel To Heal

If your relationship is making you physically ill or causing you to alter your personality then it's time to face the truth. It's time to face whatever you're afraid to face. It's time to feel whatever you've tried to bury. Maybe there are comments your spouse or loved one has said to you that you've tried to brush off or excuse, or behavior you've tried to rationalize, but if you stopped the excuses and allowed yourself to feel the pain those words and behavior have caused you, you'd be closer to healing than if you just stuffed them away. The hard feelings-- the sadness, depression, guilt, shame, fear, self-loathing, anger-- don't disappear; they just get put on layaway until one day their bill is due and the floodgates open. The manifestation of all the feelings may come at once or trickle down, but they are there and when you have the courage to face whatever cold hard truth you're afraid to face about your relationship, yourself and your life, you'll be that much closer to healing that wound.

Humanity's great capacity to love and feel loved comes with the opportunity to feel pain, yet we often choose to defer the pain or numb it with food, drugs, alcohol, sex, marathon episodes of *Keeping Up With The Kardashians*, or sadly just hardening of the heart, which in turn limits our capacity to feel, absorb and let in love. Ultimately, it is the love that will heal the pain, if we allow ourselves to feel it first. To have pain is to be human and to love and be loved is God's endowment to us.

Repeating Classes in Dating

If you ever meet a guy and think I dated him before, then you probably have. He may have a different name, race or live in a different state, but he has the same character flaws of the last jerk you dated. And that's because you didn't learn your lesson with the first guy, so you've got to date him again and again until you pass the class. I've never been a fan of math, but if I had to take Algebra II again, I'd slap someone. The key is to pay attention, learn your lesson, grow and don't repeat the class. In the past, I have dated men with self-esteem and abandonment issues. We attract the pain we're familiar with. Eckhart Tolle in *The Power Of Now* talks about pain identity and how we identify our common pain in others. Sometimes, we're even attracted to the person because he shares a similar pain. Pain identity attraction is where we usually need growth or change.

Soon after my divorce I started dating this guy named Julian. When I was married, I literally went from being a stay-at-home mom to the breadwinner within a month. My name was on the credits of a hit T.V. show every week. We had friends and relatives from all over the country calling us when one of my episodes of *Will & Grace* aired. So not only was I the breadwinner, but in a very public way. And I felt strange about my success. When I started dating Julian, I was writing for a show starring John Stamos on ABC. Julian was in between jobs and made note of the fact that I made more money than him. It was an issue that kept coming up. It became clear that Julian didn't feel good about the economic disparity and the fact that he was still trying to find his niche in the work force. I tried to assuage his feelings of inadequacy, which is an impossible task, but I also downplayed my success. At the time, I was on this career hamster wheel and though I had achieved a lot, I didn't feel as if I was enough and I measured my self-worth in my achievements. This too was a self-esteem issue that I didn't recognize. Thus, I attracted a man with the same issue: lack of self-esteem. Until I conquered that and truly felt my own worth, I kept attracting the same man and repeating the class.

I have a friend who dated two guys one black, one white and had the same experience with both. Both men were narcissists. Both men were liars. Both men impregnated another woman while in a "monogamous" relationship with my friend and of course they both lied about it. It was my friend's remarkable detective skills that unraveled the mystery behind these men's lies and forced them to eventually come clean about a portion of the truth. These boyfriends were leading double lives while dating my friend because they had other women on the side and these other women weren't just booty calls or transient encounters. The lesson my friend learned was difficult and she needed to learn it twice. She hadn't mastered it the first time so she needed to essentially repeat the class. The "never date a narcissist" class. She passed the class the second time around and should never have to repeat it again.

Recently, I dated a man who was very aggressive. He confronted people and lived aggressively. Now coming from a mid-west "make nice" background that was unfamiliar territory for me, but I had done so much growth on my own that I was ready for his "take no shit--ask for what you want--tell people about themselves attitude." And I loved this man and I loved his rough around the edges ways. I am forever grateful for the ways he emboldened me. He pushed me in situations that forced me to take my power back and to ask the hard questions and stop taking people's shit. It's been both scary and liberating, but for the first time I am walking in my own power. I'm feeling myself in a way and I will never look back, nor will I take anyone else's shit. I'll stand up for myself and my son in bigger, bolder ways that will enable us to lead not only a more authentic life, but force people to treat us better. I won't demure from asking for more money, respect and truth in every situation. No is not the worst thing that someone can say to me. And if I confront someone with the truth and get answers that are hurtful, then I'm still better off because now I know the truth about a person or situation. Knowing the truth, I can make better decisions and live my life more honestly because I was bold, daring, brave, and confrontational. Catholic High Schools administer a test: HSPT-- High School Preparedness Test. If you don't pass the test, then according to them you're not ready for high school. If you don't pass a class in dating, then you're not ready for the next level so you may have to repeat the class with another man. In my last relationship, I was ready for the confrontational, bold, daring, brave lesson of living in truth and I am forever grateful. It wasn't an easy class, but it was taught with great love, care, patience and affection.

These relationships and people whom we date can be teachers and gifts. The kinds of teachers who will not sit idle while you let others walk all over you, or don't speak your true feelings of hurt and pain. They won't let you sit in the emotional squalor and inertia we settle into when we're not living up to our highest self. These people are like the difficult teachers you had in middle school and high school who pushed you to work harder, stretched you and helped you perform at a level you never thought possible because of beliefs, doubts and fears you held about yourself. These people who cross our paths and call on us to be more, give more, and love at an authentic level are gems. Passing their classes enables us to go higher in life and love. There are lessons in both the good and bad relationships that prepare us and help us grow like nothing else can. What I've learned recently is that the relationships that end poorly and cause great suffering present the biggest opportunities for personal growth and forgiveness.

CHAPTER NINE

Men Who Go Missing

As women, we're often put in the position of waiting for a guy to show up. When he doesn't, we summon a conclave of girlfriends to analyze why we haven't heard from him until it becomes clear that he's an asshole who lied and we've been stood up. For some reason, perhaps it's the inherent care-giving aspects of our being as women to have concern for people and give them the benefit of the doubt that enables us to make excuses for men and enlist our friends to help us locate guys who have gone missing. This concern over the whereabouts of grown ass men is misdirected.

Years ago, I met a guy while visiting New York. We immediately hit it off and I discovered that he was actually from L.A., but temporarily living in New York for business. This was great news because I live in L.A. I met him the first night of my five-day excursion in New York. There was immediate flirtation. He asked for my number. He texted and called me and actually asked if he could hang out with my friends and me in the city. We had dinner with my college roommate, her boyfriend and our mutual friend. My college roommate could even sense his attraction for me. We went dancing with our mutual friend and the night before I was set to return home, he told me he'd call me once he got back to L.A. because he wanted to take me out.

He returned to L.A. a couple weeks later and he called as promised. He kept his word about wanting to take me out and we decided to have our date on a Friday night. He promised to call on Friday. As Friday waned away, I had not heard from him as promised. It was five o'clock and I started getting anxious. Was he going to call? What was happening? So I called one of my best girlfriends to get her take on the matter. She assessed that we made plans and I shouldn't assume the worst and if I had made plans with her, but hadn't heard from her by 5 p.m. that I'd call her so I should do the same and call him. I took her advice. When I called he seemed a little aloof, but said he'd been working all day and lost track of time. He asked me if I still wanted to go out tonight, which struck me as odd. I said yes. Then he asked me if I had any ideas about where to go, which I found annoying. Men, when you ask a woman out, you need to make a plan. I had encountered this wussy behavior before, but I tried to give this guy the benefit of the doubt because again he had been working all day and perhaps was exhausted from a busy workweek and couldn't think of a plan. He said he'd pick me up at 7 p.m. He had thought of a restaurant on the way over, but when he told me it was a sushi place I told him I didn't eat white rice so I hoped the restaurant had brown. Somehow this statement seemed to put him over the edge. Just because I said I didn't eat white rice, he acted like he should take me back home because he couldn't think of any other restaurant to take me to in the entire city. This was so strange. It was as if I was out with an entirely different person than I met in NYC. I assured him that despite not being able to eat white rice, I could probably find something else on the menu. We had a nice dinner, though I felt like my wit and charm kept the engine of the conversation flowing. After dinner he wanted to take me home. It was only 8:30 and I had paid for a babysitter. "Well, I guess we can go out for a drink," he said with borderline enthusiasm. The drink section of our date was better. He was more engaging and fun. Maybe it was the alcohol. We hung out at the bar a while, then he finally took me home. Now in terms of number of dates this could have been labeled as our fifth date including all of our excursions in NYC, so I invited him up, but he said he couldn't. He did offer to walk me to my door, which isn't the easiest of tasks because there is little parking on my street. He dared to double-park. He walked me to my door and gave me a big hug. Yes, a hug and kiss on the cheek. I don't need to be a CSI Investigator to figure out what that meant. I went inside and paid my babysitter more than what he paid for my half of dinner. I disseminated the date details to my girlfriends. Many of whom had differing opinions, but I concluded that this guy had probably intended on standing me up that night, but we had the mutual friend whom he might have to answer to plus I had tracked him down, made him feel guilty and forced him into half-heartedly keeping his word. That resulted in a mediocre date and time and babysitter money I can never get back. Later I found out from our mutual friend that this guy was trying to work things out with his girlfriend. So while he was pursuing me, calling, texting, asking me out, dancing with me all night, paying for my drinks, dinner etc., his real intention was to work things out with his girlfriend. That makes sense because when trying to reconcile with an ex the best approach is to pursue another woman. Needless to say, he never called me again and went missing, but stayed that way because I never tried to find his sorry, sad ass.

Here is the problem ladies, when a man goes missing do not send a search party. Tommy Lee Jones played the hell out of that FBI agent in *The Fugitive*. In fact, he won an Academy Award. Do not become Tommy Lee Jones searching every outhouse, hen house, or cathouse for the triflin' so-called man who has disappeared or not called you back. He's a grown ass man. Are we going to start putting grown ass men on milk cartons? Are we going to ask John Walsh to include guys who stand us up on *America's Most Wanted*? We don't need Amber Alerts for grown ass men. When a man gets stood up, he'll say that's interesting and move on with his day. As women, we wonder years after the broken date or the non-call was it something I said. Something I did? How did I offend him? Was it something I didn't do? Why didn't he like me? We question and doubt ourselves. We need to re-write the script to resemble something like: "I'm fantastic and he's clearly an asshole with no home-training to just stand me up."

If a man gets stood up, he won't call his friends to take a poll as to whether he should call or text his date to see if she's okay. I know because I've stood men up in the past. I have never told someone I was going to show up and then completely flaked. In one case, I called the restaurant where I was supposed to meet the guy to say that I couldn't make it. This was the early 90's before the proliferation of cell phones. I asked the hostess to relay the information, which she did. That was kind of shitty I admit it, but at least I called. That man never called me again. He never called to see what was wrong. He just went on with his life. There have been other men who have asked me out and I've canceled on them at the last minute, mostly because I had to work or write. In those cases, the men never asked me out again. They never called me. They were done because they felt they were worth more than what I was giving them. I doubt those guys called their friends and wondered and lamented over me. They moved on and that's what we need to do as women.

Be Careful Who You Stand Up

As women, we have little recourse for men who stand us up, unless we want to take to the Internet and black ball them. I'm not advocating that, but if you do it, I won't be mad at you either. Several years ago, something, I refer to as serendipitous retribution occurred when a man stood me up. I had reconnected on Facebook with this guy, Tyrell, who I had sort of dated in my twenties. He was back in town and he asked me out for a drink. We had plans to meet at 5:30 on Wednesday night. We had narrowed down our choices to two bars in Hollywood on Sunset. We agreed to decide on the bar tomorrow when he promised to call me. I gave him my phone number, but I didn't have his. We had set a date, a time and narrowed down the location to two choices. If this was not a date, then I don't know what is. And remember that he asked me out. I emailed him Wednesday afternoon, but he never responded. Once again I waited to hear from him throughout the day. This had become a telltale sign that I was going to be stood up (or, in the case of Power 106, wish that I had been stood up). Anyway, around 5:15pm, on Wednesday my girlfriend Abby called me. She said she had a random question for me. "My friend interviewed that guy Tyrell who you used to date," she said. She used Tyrell's last name, which was very unique, but I won't use his actual name here. For the sake of this story let's call him Tyrell Houdini. Abby recognized Tyrell Houdini's name when the producer told her about him. The producer, a woman, was considering hiring Tyrell for a job, but she just wished she could get someone to vouch for his character. I didn't know what to say. This was uncanny. Abby had no idea about my drinks date with Tyrell. I hadn't mentioned it to her. I literally said, "I cannot believe you're calling and asking me this today because if you had called me yesterday or a week ago I would have easily vouched for his character, but at this moment he is standing me up. We had a definite drinks date at 5:30 and it's now 5:25. He promised to call me, but he hasn't called, nor has he responded to my email." Abby said, "Everything happens for a reason. It is not just a coincidence that I'm calling you the moment he's standing you up. I'm going to tell the producer not to hire him. He's clearly not a man of his word." I felt bad because the economy was tough and people needed jobs. "Well he doesn't need this job and I know this woman is not going to hire him when I tell her your story," Abby retorted. In fact, when Abby relayed the story to the producer she said, "Hell no, he is not getting this job." She ended up hiring a woman.

So men take heed, now that over 40% of women are

breadwinners, there's a new club in town: the good old girlfriends club where women stick together. So standing up a girl can result in money out of your pocket. The old boys club that worked against us for so long is now inverted and working against the boys.

To Catch A Guy Who Never Calls Back

Not calling when one has given his word to call is bad form. It's poor manners. Clearly the man who doesn't call has not had any home training. Also, this is not a man of integrity because he cannot keep his word. This bad behavior is rampant in Hollywood. Agents, executives, managers, all sorts of industry professionals practice this unprofessional behavior daily. It's inexcusable. The Hollywood types don't call because it's sort of a power thing and if you don't have what they call "heat" in Hollywood, which just means you're a wanted commodity and making lots of money, your call may never get returned. Sometimes, industry professionals may promise to call, but then they never do--kind of like how men promise to call, but never make good on the promise. "I'll call you," becomes this passive aggressive kiss off, which is completely unnecessary. We're all adults. I may not want a man to call me or expect him to call me after a mediocre date or meeting. There's no need for men to say they are going to call unless they mean it and if they don't mean it, then don't say it. Just keep silent. The non-call answer doesn't just tell me you didn't want to talk to me again, but it also tells me you're a big, fat, pussy, lying loser. Your word doesn't mean shit. Sometimes men are afraid to let women down by not extending the mercy, "I'll call you," bit or perhaps they're afraid women will go a little crazy on them if they don't say they'll call. Here's the thing: we are not one monolithic group who all react the way your last girlfriend reacted. That being said, most adults don't appreciate being lied to. When you lie to a person, you're communicating that you don't find him or her worthy of the truth. It's after being lied to that people tend to react and can react negatively. In all deference to Steve Harvey, we wouldn't have a problem acting like ladies if these guys out here behaved like gentlemen-- honorable gentlemen who keep their word and behave with integrity.

I think a lot of us would like for these non-calling motherfellas to have to face a consequence to this triflin' behavior. I think I've come up with a pretty good one. Many of you are familiar with the former NBC correspondent Chris Hansen and the famous *Dateline NBC* show *To Catch A Predator*. I'd like someone to host a new show entitled: *To Catch A Guy Who Never Calls Back*.

Here's my pitch for the show:

Here is an example of an episode: Dan goes on a date with

Susan and it goes well. He ends the date by giving her a kiss and saying he'll call her. A week goes by and Dan has not called. We've kept him under surveillance and know that a truck has not hit him. His mother didn't die, nor did he lose his phone. Other than the fact that he lied to Susan, there is no reason why he hasn't called. It's now Saturday night and eight days since he said he'd call Susan. We have Dan under surveillance at a bar. There's a very attractive woman whom Dan is flirting with. The host and the crew watch their interaction from the other side of the bar. There is a secret microphone that picks up their conversation. The attractive woman explains to Dan that she has to get going. Dan is quick to whip out his phone and take down her number. They hug goodbye and Dan says, "I'll call you." At that moment the host with a camera crew descend upon Dan and the girl.

Host: Excuse me, you're on *To Catch A Guy Who Never Calls Back*. I'd just like to ask you a couple of questions.

Dan: What is this?

Host: We've been listening to your conversation with this woman and we heard you say that you were going to call her.

Dan: Am I on television? I don't want to be on television.

Host: Did you say you were going to call her?

Dan: Well, yeah.

Host: Are you aware of the fact that you've promised to call seven other women you've met this month, but you have yet to call any of them? And that four of those women called you and left messages and texts, but you never responded to any of them?

Dan: I don't know what you're talking about, man.

At that moment, the host removes his iPad and replays video of Dan meeting various women and telling them all he's going to call them. In one video, a woman writes her number down on a piece of paper. When she walks away, Dan crumbles it up and throws it away. Another scene plays where Dan gets out of a woman's bed, kisses her on her forehead and says, "I'll call you," before departing.

Host: You're a serial "I'll call you guy." You've lied to numerous women. What do you have to say for yourself?

Dan: Hey, I just came in here to get a beer. I wasn't trying to meet anyone or make any promises. I wasn't under oath when I said I'd call those girls.

Meanwhile, women in the bar have formed a crowd and are growing raucous and jeering at Dan. Susan emerges from the crowd.

Susan: You said you were going to call me. Liar!!!

Dan runs out of the bar. Women throw things at him.

Host: Next week we'll be featuring a sting operation on husbands who promise to fix the rain gutters, but don't. We'll uncover what they're doing instead.

Tell His Momma

My dear friend Vanessa is a realtor. She had a client, an attractive male television producer, who hired her to sell his house. There was some chemistry, but Vanessa is a woman of integrity who doesn't go around sleeping with clients. The television producer, Vince, was clearly trying to mix business and pleasure. He invited Vanessa to some of his TV business parties. She did attend. He began texting her about his house, but in time the texts became more personal. Vanessa couldn't deny her attraction and Vince didn't want her to. Finally after months of flirtation, Vanessa agreed to meet Vince for a date and sex ensued. His calls became more frequent. Flowers were delivered and Vanessa believed herself to be in a relationship. I mean, it had all the telltale relationship signs: calls, flowers, affection, dates in which he paid for everything and even a couple of sleepovers. Don't be fooled by these signs, ladies. We interpret them as signs of a relationship, but they are often confused with signs a man is pursuing a brief excursion with your lady parts and not you, nor a relationship with you. Yes, it's attached to you, but his commitment isn't to you.

Vanessa continued to believe this was at least the beginning of a relationship. She continued to be his realtor and unfortunately, Vince's house wasn't selling as quickly as they wanted. Vanessa suggested Vince hang some family pictures on the walls to make the sterile house seem homier. The next day, when Vanessa entered his home, she saw he had taken her advice and hung family photos, but what was curious was that many of the photos included an attractive woman with Vince and his family and even a couple of Vince alone with the woman. Vanessa knew Vince came from a family of two boys. Since she had been his realtor for months, she was all up in his house and this was the first evidence she found of another woman. She confronted Vince about the woman in the photos. He explained that she was an old girlfriend. Vince said that he had seen a real estate expert say on *Oprah* that if you really want your house to sell you should make it seem like a family lives there and even better a happily married couple because prospective buyers would like to inhabit a home filled with love and happiness. So he was basically just doing what Oprah said. Vanessa couldn't really argue with Oprah. Soon after that, Vince's house did sell. Now Vanessa's charge was to find him a nice rental property. During the time between finding him a new home and his move, Vince started to grow distant in terms of their relationship. There were even a couple incidents of erectile dysfunction. Now men, if you're reading this, erectile dysfunction is a mystery to us women. A mystery that we usually try to unravel with girlfriends. Yes, we do talk about your dicks with other chicks. I don't think the best source for erectile issue questions is women. I mean, if I have a question about my taxes, I'm not going to ask my gynecologist, but because we're afraid to ask you and because perhaps our girlfriends have experienced the same penile problems, we consult them. In fact one girlfriend once told me so many stories about her man's erectile dysfunction that when I met him I almost said, "I feel bad about your dick." Anyway, back to Vanessa. Vanessa told us, her girlfriends, about Vince's issues and his distance. We gave her our theories that ranged from maybe he's gay, (by the way, that is always a theory of ours) to maybe he had just jacked off right before he went out with you so things didn't work, to maybe he drank too much at dinner.

Vanessa continued to perform her duties as his realtor though Vince was unable to perform his duties in the bedroom. She found him a rental property. As is customary, when she negotiates contracts for rentals it is typical for her to include a clause that if the renter buys the property, she will receive the commission and act as realtor for the sale. Vince was adamant that he was not going to buy the property and didn't want that included in the contract. Against her better judgment, Vanessa agreed. She was feeling bad about his dick too and allowed her personal relationship with him to cloud her professional thinking. Vince did redeem himself by taking Vanessa out for her birthday and then taking her home. That night he was able to perform sexually.

Soon after the birthday date, Vanessa visited Vince at his new rental and noticed something startling. He had hanging on his walls those same family pictures featuring the old girlfriend. Oprah only said you needed to hang family/couple pictures if you're trying to sell a house, not when you're moving into a rental. When Vanessa asked him about the pictures again he said she was an old girlfriend, but a part of the family and he still sees her from time to time. All of Vanessa's red flags went up. Vince became cold and unavailable. Vanessa began to have some gynecological symptoms and went to her doctor. She found out she had an STD thanks to Vince. She tried to confront him on this, but he wouldn't take her calls and ignored her emails. He went missing. Then, to add insult to the injurious STD, Vanessa found out that Vince had hired a new realtor and made an offer on the rental house that she secured for him. Vanessa sent him a scathing email to which he responded that he did not give her the STD and that the realtor he hired was an old friend. He didn't have intentions of buying the place when he first moved in, but it grew on him. Vanessa lamented to her friends. Vince screwed her both personally and professionally and didn't even screw her well at times, we added. Yes, all the dick dysfunction excuses we had made for him earlier got degraded into limp, pencil dick, poor excuse for a man and worse. Vanessa really had no recourse to get back at Vince. If she were to file a grievance with the association of realtors, it would make her look bad professionally, especially since she didn't have anything contractual to protect herself. He had already rebuffed her calls and emails. What was she to do? I came up with a plan. I had encountered Vince earlier in my career professionally and I even knew who his mother was and where she lived. My advice to Vanessa was to write his mother a letter outlining all of his offenses, because Vince had the veneer of a nice guy with integrity who still had Sunday dinner with his family. There weren't any consequences to his bad behavior that Vanessa could inflict upon him, but if she told his mother who her son really was and attribute her lack of home training to his bad adult behavior, Vince would feel the burn of his mother's wrath for years. Sadly, Vanessa didn't take my advice. She never contacted Vince's mother. The poor woman lives in ignorance about her awful adult son. I actually wrote a screenplay about the events in which the Vince character gets his due comeuppance. If Vanessa had called his Momma, perhaps Vince's mother would have told her son off and that would have really caused him to think about himself and his behavior and change his actions with women. I don't think most men would treat women poorly if they knew it could get back to their mothers. And hopefully Vanessa's actions would go viral on the Internet, which would cause many more men to think before they cheated, lied, or acted disrespectfully toward women.

CHAPTER TEN

Breaking Up Is Hard To Do, But Getting Dumped Can Suck It!

We're all familiar with the song "Love Don't Live Here Anymore." The lyrics tell us that there's a vacancy because there's no love anymore. We often don't fall out of love so much as get pushed out, evicted, or asked to leave in not so many words. Sometimes there aren't words at all, but silence. A silent love eviction notice doesn't make sense, but neither does the actual fall into love, so why should the fall out be logical. If there are no words, sometimes we read the clues by actions or inactions, subtle differences in the way he used to touch you, talk to you and make you feel like you're his only need. The love-leaving feeling is just that: a feeling. A knowing in the heart that the end stages are near. It would be nice if there were a hospice worker and pamphlet to guide you through this end journey and show you the death rattle signs. The thing is we see the signs, but we do a denial dance hoping they will dissipate so we can live in the love longer. But if we listen to our gift of fear and intuitive leads, we truly know that eviction is imminent. How we handle a break-up is a testimony about one's character.

It's important that when being evicted from love and a relationship that you do so with grace and trust. Trust that this isn't the right fit for you. Yes, it was right for a while and you may think that you can still make it right, that you can change, or be the way you used to be, or be a new way he wants you to be, or just hold him so tight that he can't leave, which is akin to imprisonment. And we all know that's not love so much as felony kidnapping. You need courage on both sides of a break-up. The courage to see another day and the courage to stay away from your ex. Music has been proven to help people deal with illness. I know cancer patients who have playlists for chemo. Music can also help you through a break-up. Make yourself a break-up play list. Miranda Lambert's "Mama's Broken Heart" is the battle hymn of the republic for jilted ladies. If love knocks you off your feet, Kelly Clarkson has a fight song to get you back into the game: "Stronger," "Since You Been Gone." Breaking up is shitty and you need a village to get you through, but the good news is every day is a once in a lifetime experience, even the shitty days. So thank God you won't experience those days over and over. The pain will be different from day to day. It's the moments after an earthquake that are the scariest and most fragile. But months later, after the rebuilding has begun, the shock of the event rests deeper inside of us and life has continued. And somewhere around the fifth month the pain of those first post love eviction days will be a distant memory. The pain will be erased almost like childbirth pain that seems to be something women can compartmentalize enough to go through labor many times over and not allow the fear of the re-experiencing the labor pains dissuade them from giving birth again. You will fall in love again and you may even get evicted from love again, but the cost benefit analysis will always prove it's a risk worth taking. It's the ultimate, singular human experience that makes us feel alive and wanted. When one is fully present in the love, it is EVERYTHING. So if you've been evicted from love, gracefully step down as Miss America does every year. Wave goodbye, shed a few tears and trust and believe that this won't be the last time you wear the crown. Now there is a vacancy but believe that your heart will be filled again. Listen to your play list, learn from your mistakes and dare to love again. Become your own encourager in dating and life. Stay strong and stay away from your ex to avoid a backsliding break-up.

In those hours, days and weeks following a break-up both parties are vulnerable and weak. Like newly sober addicts who long for their drug, people who get dumped long for one last fix with their ex. I'm talking break-up sex. I know many people who partake in break-up sex as a means to cut the cord. Now that doesn't make any sense. If you think about it practically speaking how can you cut the cord when it's inserted in you again. I would advise against break-up sex. I'm not sitting in judgment. It happens. But sex with the ex is a gateway drug that leads you back into the throws of a bad or mediocre relationship. T.I. raps so eloquently in "No Mediocre," well we shouldn't want mediocre either. None of us should want a mediocre anything. Sex with the ex leads to compromise. If you broke up with your man because he couldn't commit, but now find yourself having sex with him again and in a quasi relationship, you have compromised. You lie to yourself and say it's different, or I can handle casual sex with a man who has been the cornerstone of my marital fantasies for the past three years. You convince yourself that you don't want a ring anymore. You tell yourself that you're the cool girl, who doesn't care if she's being used, or shat upon or taken for granted. Do not go down the break-up sex road. Phone a friend or call a lifeline if you need help resisting. And if you really need to get sex off your brain, call your grandmother. Talk through the break-up with her.

The thing about break-up sex is it's usually secret. We don't tell our friends about it until much later. We have no real accountability with break-up behavior. Unlike when you leave a job, there is no exit interview to analyze the relationship with a neutral third party who can shed some light on why you have to uncouple and find something new. Unless you have a therapist, you're left analyzing with girlfriends, or just mulling it over in your head a million times. Here is my remedy for that. Imagine your relationship exit interview with Charlie Rose, or a Charlie Rose-like anchor. Charlie Rose will analyze your dating career like he would a movie or an international crisis. He'll ask the tough questions and expose the ugly underbelly to the relationship and why leaving is the only solution.

Snippet From Charlie Rose Relationship Exit Interview (imagined Charlie Rose dialogue)

WOMAN: He forgot my birthday Charlie, and promised to make up for it, but never really did. We went away to Vegas for a long weekend, which was kind of supposed to be my belated birthday present. When we got to Vegas his credit card got declined so I ended up paying for the entire trip. He never paid me back.

IMAGINED CHARLIE ROSE: It's really despicable what he's done to you, but what is more tragic here is what you've allowed him to do. Where is the self-respect? I think what we have here is a portrait of a lady being used.

WOMAN: You're right, Charlie. He really wasn't good to

me or for me. Plus, he sometimes had trouble maintaining an erection. I'm better off without him.

IMAGINED CHARLIE ROSE: This break-up seems more like a breakthrough.

WOMAN: Charlie Rose, you are so wise and dashing. Would you want to go out with me?

Okay do not ask Charlie Rose out during your break-up exit interview, but do realize that when someone walks away from you it's not your job to chase after him. Just say goodbye and open up your heart and your life to the person who is walking towards you.

A Stevie Wonder Song

Have you ever listened to the lyrics of most any Stevie Wonder song, but more specifically "You Are The Sunshine Of My Life?" Don't we all want someone to regard us as the sunshine of their life and tie a "ribbon in the sky for our love?" Mediocre relationships and liaisons don't warrant such melodic tunes that transport you to another worldly location where love reigns supreme. Dare to dream of the possibility that someone will even hear a Stevie Wonder song and have loving thoughts of you. Stop being stand-in girl. The girl who some guy was in closest proximity to at last call. The girl who answered the phone at two in the morning. The side-piece girl who agreed to shelve her dreams and her desire to be truly, rightly, and fully loved. Don't be the girl who is looking at some loser next to her on the couch wondering when she stopped believing in love and settling for second-hand companionship out of desperation and loneliness.

Profound loneliness is real. It hurts. It cries out in a quiet desperate, shameful pain, afraid to admit its truth. The irony is it's not alone. So many know that pain, but cover it up with someone in their arms for whom they feel little to nothing. Breaking up requires strength, hope and belief that one day, as a self-assured woman, you can have the kind of "For Once In My Life" -- Stevie Wonder kind of love.

The Top 5 Warning Signs It's Time To Get Out Of A Relationship or Marriage

1. You can only have sex with your husband while fantasizing that he's Justin Timberlake, Usher or Channing Tatum. And now you actually scream their names out during sex with your man, but make no apologies.
2. When your man leaves on a trip and you wonder aloud that if his plane crashes and he dies that may not be such a bad thing. You go online to shop for your funeral dress.

3. When you have more affection for your cleaning lady than him.
4. When you start to rationalize and tell yourself things are not that bad and no one is really happy, no one has sex anymore. You've become accustomed to living in misery.
5. When you say to yourself, yes my relationship is bad, but at least I'm not single. When did single become so awful? Sarah Jessica Parker and all her friends in the city had fun for about six seasons and two feature films. So the fun continues.

Proper, Healthy Ways to Handle a Break-Up

1. Listen to a Beyoncé song. If he lied, cheated, or left you, Beyoncé has a song for that and a national anthem for your new state of singleness.
2. Summon a conclave of girlfriends to privately bash him and drink to excess.
3. Get dressed up; go to a club or bar, make-out with a hot stranger. You don't even have to know his name just make sure he doesn't have any cold sores.
4. Change your Facebook status to: happy, hot, single and ready to mingle. Can I get a "what, what"?
5. Meditate, love yourself and pray for someone better.

6. Make a list of the things you want in your life then go get them for yourself rather than wait for a man to bring them in a relationship.

How to Handle a Break-Up in an Unhealthy Way (Please don't do these things, but some of them may be nice to fantasize about)

1. Bash him on the Internet. Set up a webpage and a twitter account dedicated to taking him down, exposing his misdeeds, his sexual deficiencies and spread a rumor that he wears a toupee and weeps after sex. Do the same on his Facebook page and include photoshopped pictures of him crying.
2. "Take a Louisville slugger to both head-lights, carve your name into his leather seats" and everything else Carrie Underwood sung about.
3. Follow him onto a date and tell the new woman of his misdeeds, and his habitual premature ejaculation. So premature that it's prior to penetration. He's not the only one crying after an attempt at sex and that's really all it ever was a failed attempt.
4. Call him and harass him at home, work, his gym or just out on the street.
5. Refuse to bathe, get out of bed, drink, eat, or take drugs to numb the pain for more than two weeks. And vow to never love again.

CHAPTER ELEVEN
Tennis, Love and the Truth

I have this dear friend, Eloise; she may be the smartest friend I have. She's an intellectual. She's practical. She looks at things empirically. She budgets. She makes thoughtful researched decisions in everything, except love. When it comes to relationships and love, Eloise is all heart. She's romance, poetry and fantasies. In fact, she's read poetry aloud with past boyfriends. She described the first three months of her time with one boyfriend as being beautiful. The entire 90 day probationary period of the relationship was romantic and beautiful. When a boyfriend sent me roses on Valentine's Day, she was the friend who swooned and was even more joyful than me. She gazed at the flowers, admired their beauty and gave my boyfriend lots of points that day. Eloise is a true romantic. Date night, Valentine's Day, birthdays and every holiday in between require a special plan, and night and gifts and a celebration for her. And that is great... for her. Hopefully it also works out for the guy she dates and finally marries. My theory about relationships doesn't jibe with the romantic movie version that many women hold dear. My friend Eloise understands the practicality of everyday relationships, but she still needs the beauty. I believe that the beauty and romance only fulfill about 12% of an entire relationship. For me, relationships and marriage are about the everyday grind.

I come from a family of tennis fans and players. My mom has been playing tennis forever. I spent springs and summers growing up in Cleveland at tennis courts playing with other tennis players' kids at nearby parks. I've been playing since childhood. One of the first autobiographies I read was by my favorite tennis player, Chris Everett. I've been watching Wimbledon and US Open coverage with my family since I was a kid. In the summer of 1999, as an adult, I had my tonsils removed. The pain involved was off the charts. Whenever I swallowed anything it felt like razor blades were going down my throat. I couldn't eat. It was the best diet ever. I lost nine pounds in six days. During this same time, Pete Sampras was playing at Wimbledon and I'm a big Pete fan. This was towards the end of his career and though he was a favorite at the championships at Wimbledon, there were those who didn't think he could win another major tournament. Anyway, as I struggled to recover and heal from this surgery and find little things to eat every day that didn't cause my throat to bleed and increase my pain, I likened my journey to Pete Sampras' Wimbledon fortnight. In fact, I told myself that if Pete could make it to the finals and win, I could get through this pain and recover from my surgery. Every day and then every other day, Pete battled opponents losing some points, but always winning more. There were times when he looked out of the set, but he always came back. Through hard work, dedication, perseverance, sweat and belief, Pete Sampras won the Wimbledon title that year. Through belief, perseverance and dedication to recover, I made it through that grueling post-op two-week period. At the end of the two weeks, I was back on solid food. The pain had noticeably subsided and I was on my way back to normalcy.

The score of love is unique to the game of tennis, but it's not the score you want because it means zero. Love and relationships are a lot like tennis. We're practicing, working, grinding through the everyday with our partner. We're weathering storms, dysfunction, insecurities, deaths, and loss. There are valleys, mountaintops and of course the time in between, which is where we spend the majority of our life. So yes, I watched Pete Sampras battle through seven matches to get to the point where he could hold up the big trophy at the end, but that trophy moment, the moment of pomp and circumstance, and the red carpet moment do not show us how Pete got there, it just shows us the peak of his journey.

People love to watch championships. They love to watch the pinnacle of an athlete's season. The Superbowl remains the highest rated sports program, but the lesser fans don't watch all the weekly games and no one watches the practices. The reality is an athlete will spend more time practicing than he or she ever will spend on the winner's podium. That romantic, joyful moment is fleeting. That's the same 12% romance of a relationship that I referred to earlier.

When I see players break down after winning Wimbledon, I cry with them because I know the sacrifice, the dedication, the perseverance, the blood, sweat, and tears that it takes to get to that point. There is as much to be learned from a big loss as there is from a win. Losses can be educational and are fuel to take you to the next game and hopefully to a win. My dad played on the undefeated 1972 Dolphins team. His team went 17 and 0 that year and won the Superbowl, but the year before the team lost in a crushing defeat at the Superbowl. At the end of that defeat, they began their quest to reach and win at the Superbowl the following year. I live in Los Angeles where in the past The Lakers have been a winning franchise. The Lakers and L.A. have been described as fostering a culture of winning. Until recently, The Clippers were not a winning team. There were empty seats and a Clippers ticket was never hard to get, but once they acquired Chis Paul and began winning that changed. Everyone likes winners and success, but to get to that point there is a journey that involves loss. It is the climb just like the Miley Cyrus song. Yes, I'm a 40 something year-old woman and I just quoted Hannah Montana. Deal with it. And I say Hannah Montana because I liked her better then. Those romantic moments are beautiful, as Eloise says, and we all long for those moments, but they are not the everyday reality, the journey, the climb and truth of any long-term relationship. It's the everyday moments, the grind that gets us to the top.

    I'm not much of a romantic. Don't get me wrong, I loved receiving roses from one of my boyfriends on Valentine's Day. I also love and appreciate the ordinary moments in my past relationships. I don't look at a relationship as just what I can get out of it. Athletes don't dedicate and sacrifice themselves and their bodies just to get the accolades and the trophies. It's a give and take relationship. The sacrifice they put into it comes back to them, but it's their love for the sport that enables them to sacrifice. The same is true for loving relationships. To paraphrase our 35th president John F. Kennedy: we need to ask not what our husbands and boyfriends can do for us, but ask more of what we can do for our loved ones because it will come back to us. Loving sacrifices don't feel as if we're giving something up. They feel as if we're sewing into the life of our beloved and that's mutually beneficial.

A Movie Kiss

During one particular season of *Sex and The City*, Carrie Bradshaw was dating a guy named Berger. There was trouble in this relationship, but they were trying to hang onto it and make it work. In one scene, Carrie and Berger weren't agreeing and to nullify the moment, Berger said they needed a Hollywood kiss. A Hollywood kiss is a dramatic public kiss where Berger bent Carrie over and planted one on her lips. Their relationship ended later in that episode. Relationships aren't made on movie kisses alone.

Movie kisses are fake kisses between actors who are being paid to act romantic. Romance is nice, but we need to recalibrate our expectations. If you haven't put in the work and absorbed losses but persevered then you're not going to make it to the winners circle at Wimbledon. Well the same is true for love. That movie kiss will mean so much more when you and your mate have weathered storms and come to the brink of calling it quits, but found a way to work at your relationship and get it back on track. Ben Affleck got some flack for an award acceptance speech, in which he referred to his marriage as work, but the truth is that relationships and marriages are work. We like to idealize them and have this misconception that they are not supposed to be work, that they are supposed to be full of beauty, but even beauty needs maintenance.

When we only see results and not the work that goes into something, it's deceptive. We'd be better served watching moments of conflict resolutions from real marriages and relationships than another Jennifer Lopez or Kate Hudson romantic comedy. The moments of beauty, elation, and joy my friend Eloise longs for should be felt and absorbed, but they are fleeting. Marriage and relationships can be the most intense bonds we ever share with another human being. Your mate is not always going to say and be what you want or need them to be which is why we shouldn't put that much pressure on that one person to be our everything, to solve all our past problems, insecurities and make our imperfections perfect.

Tennis players often battle themselves on the court. Sometimes our biggest obstacles in relationships are not our spouse or boyfriend, but ourselves. Our stories. How were we loved or not loved by our parents? How did our previous husband, wife or significant other mistreat us? How do we feel about ourselves? Do we feel deserving of real unconditional love? Do we fear abandonment or commitment? In tennis, commentators often say only Serena Williams can beat Serena Williams. She has the all around game. She possesses the fastest serve in women's tennis. She can move, has a fierce net game and can always come back from behind. So when Serena loses it's stunning and the experts and commentators give some credit to her opponent, but her losses are often attributed to her not playing her best because when she's at her best she's unbeatable. Sometimes we beat ourselves out of loving, fulfilling, beautiful relationships because we lack belief, we get in our heads and we talk ourselves out of the game.

Head Cases

Some tennis players who have left the game didn't leave because they were injured or physically unable to play anymore, but left because they became what some in the sport refer to as a head case. In the game of tennis, we often see the players go into their corners on the court and talk to themselves. Sometimes they scream or curse at themselves. Others throw racquets and many are known for having full-blown tantrums. Maria Sharapova is known to take quiet moments in between points to pick at her racquet strings and focus. This occurs between her often-rhythmic grunts during points. Tennis is a very mental game. After Andy Murray won Wimbledon, he talked about the mental exhaustion of playing in such a high intensity and pressure filled match. Momentum changes in tennis matches as it does in relationships and in life and even when you're down, you have to be able to stay up and fight in the game and in your relationship. A tennis player has to play every point and be present in each point. She can't be thinking about the next match. When tennis players become head cases their thoughts spiral out of control. They start over-thinking, doubting, rushing and losing confidence. To win a championship it takes hard work, heart, guts, joy, belief and trust. Players are told to play their own game. Be authentic. Can you see how these same principles apply to love and relationships? If you doubt that your relationship is going to work out, it doesn't have a fighting chance. If you work hard, sacrifice, are true to who you are, love with your whole heart, have guts and trust your gut, enjoy the experience, be confident, have faith and don't over think things then you do have a chance at love.

Here is how we become head cases in dating. And I speak from first hand dating head case experience. Let's say you've been dating a guy for months maybe over a year and he seems distant lately. He isn't calling as much and you immediately think it's about you. Suddenly your thoughts are spinning out of control. He doesn't love you anymore. He's found someone else. When you made that royal wedding reference, he thought you were pressuring him to get married. Maybe he is gay? You keep yourself up at night thinking that it's all about you. Not once have you entertained the idea that maybe there's something going on with him that has nothing to do with you. Before you met this man he'd been living a life with a career, a family, friends, hobbies. Perhaps his world doesn't revolve around you. Perhaps you should ask him if there is anything wrong instead of becoming a head case. Maybe he's crazed at work, or he got into a misunderstanding with his mom, or his best friend needs a big loan. You won't know until you ask. And you won't be able to move forward if you continue with the out of control negative thoughts. Negative thoughts hardly ever lead to positive thoughts. Negative thoughts are like cancer cells that just multiply and make you sicker until they get excised from your brain. If you're a head case, you'll never be a champion at love because your head will keep you out of the game. And in love the prizes are not trophies and money, but are a series of everyday moments that make you feel less alone; the hug at the end of a tough week, the smile that warms you like the sun, and the other hand to hold as you journey through life together. If we treasure those moments, we'll feel like champions every day.

There Are No Rules Only Guidelines

I have a white girlfriend who always dated black men, but then chose to marry a white man. Yes, she chose to defy the saying: "Once you go black you never go back." She was married to this white guy for many, many years, then divorced him and went right back to dating black men. Because the saying is not just a saying, it's the truth. I know a Jewish guy who was not that attracted to Jewish women, but married one anyway to please his mother. The problem is that your mother will eventually die and then you're left with this life long choice you made to please her, to meet her or society's standard of what your life should look like and who you should be. We need to re-write the rules and create our own for dating and life so that we don't choose people who adhere to others' standards.

Though I believe there are some universal red flags in relationships, what may be a red flag for one woman could be a welcome mat for another. We're all unique and so is each relationship. One woman's quirks may attract a guy who sits on her couch and does nothing and she's okay with that. While another woman will not stand for that behavior and feel the compulsion to set the couch on fire while her man is still sitting on it, like Farrah Fawcett's character from *The Burning Bed* (though in Farrah's case it was the bed she set on fire). We shouldn't judge each other, unless of course you do commit a crime like the latter example and then a jury of your peers will judge you. And by the way Farrah Fawcett's character was found not guilty. #Imjustsayin. But please, ladies, let's not ever get to the point where one even contemplates burning a bed. Please obey the laws of the land despite being in a terrible marriage. There's always another way out. And if you make a choice that is true to you and not someone else, hopefully you won't even contemplate burning the bed. You still may want to hit your man upside his head with a frying pan, but everybody has that fantasy.

Why I Wear My Bite Guard to Bed Even if There is Impending Sex

It's not just because my officious, sometimes scary, heavily accented German dentist warned me against losing my teeth to my own grinding; I wear it religiously because I follow rules. I pay my taxes. I paid my alimony. I didn't commit adultery. I obey traffic rules. I feel bad when I tip 12%. That said, here is what I've learned in life: it doesn't pay to follow all the rules all of the time. Some of the rules can work for you, but others work against you. Many of the rules I'm referring to are not laws, but "old wives' tale" type of rules set up by society as a means to guide one's life.

One familiar relationship rule is to let men be men and let women be women. My interpretation of that rule is that as women we should probably not be hunters and gatherers because that upsets the relationship ecosystem, though there are many women out-earning their men and they find a way to make it work, so that rule doesn't completely apply to all. I do think men still need to be hunters and gatherers in other aspects of the relationship though. If we think there are relationship rules that apply to every relationship then we're screwed. Every relationship, like the stars in the sky and the hairs on your head and the zits on your chin, is unique. So when we assume that the unwritten rules of relationships apply to ours, but for some reason our man is not behaving as we think he should according to the rules, then we assume there is something wrong with our relationship. When our girl's man is calling her every night before he goes to bed, but our man isn't, we assume there is something wrong with "us" as a couple. When you see other couples who are outwardly affectionate, but your guy isn't, you think there's something wrong, but looks can be deceiving. What is on the outside and measured by someone else's standards shouldn't mean shit to you.

I've had friends tell me about boyfriends and preface their introduction with caveats: I know he's too old or too young for me, or not good-looking enough, or too attractive, or fat or thin, or blonde, or black or half Asian, or doesn't make much money, or too rich. What the eff?! So what? Who says you can't like someone because he's younger than you, or older than you or doesn't have a car? These are rules we've made up in our head or heard on the street that have no valid application in our lives since our lives don't abide by rules. Our lives don't even abide by our rules or dreams or guidelines or life-plans so why would they stay in the lane of other people's rules or expectations? I've already established that people in general don't expect great things so why would we try to fit our life to adhere to a flawed human race that doesn't even expect the best. Let's stop the insanity and throw out the invisible rulebook, but hold onto this book because it's funny, entertaining and will make you think.

I may wear my bite guard to bed every night and even on red-eye flights, but that rule is just for me because I'm a little paranoid and a part time hypochondriac. That does not mean that everyone has to follow my rule or any rule for life. I am not advocating NOT following traffic rules. Those are good ones that should not be left up to interpretation, even though people do it every day. There are no relationship rules. Every relationship is different. When boundaries are broken or crossed that feel wrong in your heart and your gut, then it may be time to end a relationship, but not when your friend or friends think he's not living up to their rules and expectations. What are their rules based upon anyway? Their rules are probably based upon their family of origin. Families are like embassies. Once you step into an embassy, you have stepped onto foreign soil. Foreign countries like families have all sorts of different doctrine, rules and culture. Others' rules aside, you are the only one who knows your heart and gut. Hopefully, I've given you some stories, guidelines, warnings, red-lights, thoughts and some of my own rules to ponder and if they ring true pay attention and if they don't turn the page, but only you know you. And if you don't know yourself, I suggest you get to know you before joining together in matrimony, engagement, living in sin or just hanging out with someone else.

PART TWO

CHAPTER TWELVE

Desperation in Life and Love

"Can you remember who you were before the world told you who you should be?"
Danielle La Porte

Look, over the years I've done some digging--a sort of life excavation--and what I learned about love, marriage, divorce and almost everything else is that if the dating thing isn't working in your life it may be a symptom that your life is not working overall. How I allowed myself to be treated in romantic relationships often mimicked how I allowed myself to be treated in my career. I'm still working through the pain, but I feel closer to my Promised Land, which is just the place of knowing I am enough; I am fully loved and I am a worthy. Hopefully my journey will help you get to yours.

Dating can be a difficult and arduous journey. There are times that I've been desperate in life and love. After writing for *Will & Grace*, I wrote for another comedy on ABC: *Jake in*

Progress starring John Stamos. That show was short-lived and once the axe of cancellation fell, I found myself unemployed and several months away from when new TV staffing period would begin. So I needed a job. Despite having great credits and great samples, I was getting desperate and would have settled for anything. A show that was interested in me, but before I had a meeting there, my agent told them I was taking my time reading scripts and being very selective about my next endeavor. That was a position of power, which made me more desirable, not desperate. That was also a lie. The truth was: I was unemployed, with a child, a mortgage and alimony payments, so I <u>really</u> needed a job. Let's put it this way, if Jimmy Fallon were offering to pay me $100 and a chicken dinner for a joke, I would have taken it and I don't even like chicken. But the attitude my agent conveyed made me more desirable so that the people who wanted me had to work harder and make me a fantastic offer to get me on their team. It's not about playing hard to get. It's about believing that you are worth someone working hard to get you, whether it's in business and especially in love.

Public Love, Public Loss

I had this big wedding and when you do that you kind of put your relationship on public display. The wedding couple is photographed going through the rituals of the first dance, kiss, and feeding each other cake while onlookers watch them the way people watch animals in the zoo or admire works of art behind glass. As a former bride, I can attest to the fact that in some way you know people are watching and so you're acting a little bit. It's less Meryl Streep acting and more Tori Spelling performing for the reality cameras acting. You're playing the role of a beautiful, happy bride because that's what's expected and you're being asked to put your private love on public display. It's weird because you don't normally feed your spouse cake while being photographed or dance as hundreds of people watch you, but we've been conditioned through society to mimic how couples act in situations like that from seeing them in movies, television, reading about it and then going to weddings and watching how that scene plays out in real life.

So it only makes sense that because I put my love on display, my divorce was also made available for public viewing. There's something about getting a divorce that opens you up for public scrutiny. It was as if I had a wake with a viewing for the death of my marriage so everyone could look in the casket and form an opinion. In fact, there have been points in my life when I've felt like a human blog with unwelcome visitors who felt entitled to leave a comment on my missteps in life: how they knew my marriage was never going to work out; who I should be dating now; what type of job I should try to get; what I should really be writing; how to raise my child; why my son's life is going to be difficult because I got a divorce. Clearly, I did something horrifically wrong, hence my divorce; therefore, it is open season for people to dole out their judgment and amateur life coaching advice to moi. And guess what...? I'm really sick of it. I know they mean well, but I don't care. Maybe they are dead wrong. There is a chance that I'm more awake to my life, my heart, and my dreams than the average married person. Maybe I'm courageous enough to get out of a bad marriage and take a chance on myself. Maybe I understand that I cannot continue in a career that is mind numbing and I have enough faith to step out and try something new. Maybe I'm not afraid if I don't drive the fancy car or live in the expensive mini-mansion because it means that I'll be enslaved to a bank or a corporation that is just slowly killing me. Maybe I'm just human, fallible and trying to figure my life out just like everyone else. Just because I'm trying and failing by some ridiculous standard, but my so-called failings have been made public, doesn't mean I've extended an invitation for anyone to openly criticize my life and my choices. Perhaps my so-called failures are my route to success.

    Married people seem immune to the harsh scrutiny that the divorced and single receive. I guess because while married it seems like you must be doing something right because there is this other person who has endorsed you for as long as you both shall live. The truth behind the closed doors of that marital endorsement could be extremely vile. I've seen it. I know married people who hate each other more than I ever disliked my ex. In fact, there is more love between my ex and me now as divorced people than there is between some married folks I know. I know women who are more in love with their house and their zip code than their husband, but the husband pays for the house so they keep him around. I know marriages that require copious amounts of wine in order to stay intact. I know some husbands who should sleep with one eye open because their wives have so much venom that I'm afraid for them. I know wives who are just waiting around for their husbands to die, praying that a really bad flu season could help along their cause. I know married people who haven't killed each other only because they are both law-abiding citizens and their fear of prison outweighs their murderous desires.

One has to get to a place in life where no one's opinion matters, especially your mother's or best friend's, or any other person who is asserting his or her own opinion as gospel and expertise on your life. They may mean well, but they are not you. The sage Dr. Wayne Dyer advises people "to be independent of the good opinion of others." If you passed your divorce/break-up exam, guess what? You got your Ph.D. in yourself, so if anyone is an expert, it is YOU. Ignore the public scrutiny because it's less about you and more about the scrutinizer.

Scrutiny says: I'm smarter than you; I'm better than you; you don't know what you're doing with your life. I pity you.

Mother Theresa said, "If you judge people, you have no time to love them." Operating from a deficit of love breeds fear. The scrutiny that has been visited upon others and me is really about fear. The one who is fearful is the scrutinizer. Even though it seems as if divorce is at epidemic proportions, those who choose divorce are still breaking with conventions of society - a society in which marriage is an institution. When I told married friends, co-workers or acquaintances that I was getting a divorce, I was often met by a bizarre reaction. People had the audacity to tell me that I shouldn't get divorced. Some people even inserted their moral code into my situation. One co-worker asked me if my husband had cheated on me. When I told her no, she then attempted to tell me that my marriage could be saved. Apparently, infidelity was her marriage deal-breaker. Again, we have an instance of someone asserting her opinion and judgment onto my life. Another friend of my husband's told me that he and his wife had major problems too, but they weren't getting a divorce hence I should be able to stick it out as well. Some people asked me for reasons why I was getting a divorce. It was as if I had to qualify it for them and get them to sign off on my decision. A friend's mother told her to tell me that I should not get divorced. She said my decision was wrong and went against God.

Since I was a divorce pioneer amongst my friends, years later when I had close friends make the tough decision to divorce, a couple of their husbands blamed my influence upon their wives. Literally, some of the now ex-husbands said their wives only wanted a divorce because they had been hanging around me and I was divorced. I guess they thought it was contagious. Somehow I had rubbed off on them and made divorce more palatable. All of these reactions to my very personal decision were fear based. The end of my marriage exposed the fragility and vulnerability of their own marriages. Their reactions were a defensive attempt to annihilate my apparent disregard for an institution where they had put their faith and trust. My decision to leave for the hope of something better didn't jibe with the rationalizations and bargaining these other married people were making every day so they could stay in their dysfunctional unions. My courage and faith to leave spat in the face of their fear and complacency that held them captive. I'm not advocating that people wantonly leave their marriages, but staying in a relationship because you're afraid to leave is not life affirming. Marriage should be taken seriously. The actual institution should not be deified to the point that one stays in a union that is harmful, abusive and suffocating.

Those who muster up enough courage and bravery to end an unhealthy relationship or quit their jobs, which are enslaving or are fired and dare to do something new and different, are mavericks and innovators. But society doesn't recognize them as mavericks or innovators until they invent something and are successful or remarry the so-called perfect person. The time in between failure and success is the most fragile time for these courageous individuals who have stepped out on faith. It's the time that they most need love and compassion and the space to fulfill their destiny.

CHAPTER THIRTEEN
Fear, Faith & Being Single

What I've learned from dating, from relationships that didn't work out and from my divorce is that I applied the same principles to my romantic life as I did to my professional life. If I'm being completely honest with myself, I've dated and even married out of fear. Fear that this might be the only guy who will ask me out so I might as well go out with him. Fear that even though he doesn't treat me the way I want him to there might not be anyone out there who treats me any better so I might as well stick with him. Fear that this may be my only shot at getting married and I already bought the wedding dress and people are flying in from out of town so I don't want to let anyone down. Fear that if I don't go out with him, I'll be alone on New Year's Eve. Fear is inverted faith, and I lacked faith in dating and in my career. Ultimately, I learned that I lacked faith in myself.

Single does not necessarily mean alone and lonely. There

were times in my marriage or in a committed relationship where I felt more alone than ever. The sting of loneliness is exacerbated when you're supposed to be in a wedded union with another human being, but there is no unity. Loneliness hides behind relationships that aren't working -- the ones that don't provide love, support or edification or even offer a sliver of joy. These false fear-driven unions perpetuate that mask that keeps loneliness at bay and true love out of reach. I will say I've felt the depths of my most profound loneliness, while in false unions, mostly because when coupled there is this notion that one is not supposed to feel alone.

I had a serious boyfriend in college and there were times in the months preceding our break-up when we'd go out into the world and pose as a happy couple, but once out of the public lens, we'd retreat home to our neutral corners of isolation. That's when I've felt most alone; those times when the world has viewed me as Mrs. or someone's girlfriend. I may have had the title, but it was slipping away from me. I was trying to hold onto a relationship that had died. The title was a formality, but it communicated to the world that I wasn't alone, even though I knew I was. Many of us are holding onto the Mrs. title or the girlfriend, husband, wife or domestic partner title. We work hard to get those titles. In some cases, we have official government paperwork to prove our title so I understand why it's difficult to part with them. Many of us are holding onto marital titles like an aged, out of shape, Heavy Weight Champion of the World title. Heavy Weight Champion of the World is such a grand title I understand why they fight to the near death for it, but when it's over, when it's clear that you're past your prime, that you're trying to hold onto past glory and unable to face present defeat, isn't it better to surrender with grace, dignity and the preserved memory of your championship days than go into a ring on an international stage and have someone beat your ass? That's what many people in lifeless marriages and relationships are trying to do: hold on desperately to a title. The title is not the essence of who you are. The title doesn't represent the state of affairs in your marriage. The title is for public consumption. The title is about ego and pride.

You can be single and surrounded by love and be fully loved and you can be married and facing a depleted love tank every day. It's not even running on the fumes of kindness. It's void of anything benevolent. So don't be fooled by what marriages and relationships and people with marital titles look like on the outside. Don't underestimate your ability to be happy as a single person. Many people are staying in *Bridges Of Madison County*--like marriages waiting for a younger, dashing Clint Eastwood-- maybe his son Scott Eastwood -- to come in for a long weekend and steal them away from their stale unions and give them a glimpse of passion and love. Or people are reading

Fifty Shades of Grey to partake in a vicarious, dangerous, erotic thrill away from their bland, mundane, decayed marital sex lives or their complete absence of sex. Don't stay in a relationship past its prime because of fear of the unknown. The unknown could be so much better than the known you're living in today.

Some people stay in relationships past its expiration date because they become comfortable in their complacency. This applies to all life situations. In the beginning, when the marriage started to go bad, there was extreme discomfort, but when the situation didn't change, an adaptation took place. A metaphorical opposable thumb grew out of the marital discord that enabled the unhappy spouse to adapt to unhappiness to the point that he or she doesn't feel unhappy anymore. They have adapted to the new normal of living in a bad marriage. They've accepted that things are not going to change. These comfortably complacent people are lying to themselves. They are like hoarders who no longer see the squalor and filth they abide in and call home. They build a wall around their heart to guard from really feeling anything and put blinders on their eyes so they can't see the truth. They are comfortable and complacent in their filth and have abandoned hopes for something better. Expiration dates are there to protect us. We would never drink spoiled, curd-filled, nasty, old milk yet we'll stay in a decaying relationship.

I know people who stay in relationships because they are afraid of the mess and chaos that will be created if they leave, but I don't understand this philosophy. These people are choosing to stagnate. They are immobilized in their fear of what could be. There could be chaos, a storm, or there could be smooth sailing above the clouds. There could be a return to life. There could be mind-blowing passionate sex, love and intimacy beyond what you could think or imagine, especially in light of the conjugal, marital sex you've been having or not having for years.

Don't be afraid of the storms in life. Your fear will trap you in the eye of the tornado that's just passing through. Your faith will keep you rooted as the storm passes. Faith is a courageous endeavor in the eye of the storm, but if you close your eyes, stop looking at the tornado of your life and cling to the hope of a brighter future, the storm will pass and you'll be left standing stronger than ever.

A break-up or divorce may seem like the worst storm ever and it may have you in a ditch of depression, emotional chaos or financial Armageddon, but this is not the worst thing in the world and if you are open to what life, spirit and God have to show you about yourself, this may be the best thing to ever happen to you.

It's not the storm or the natural disaster of your life that makes you stronger. We don't necessarily have to endure a bad thing to get to something good. It's one's ability to survive the disaster that demonstrates the strength one already possesses. When people say you are stronger than you know, it is that strength they are speaking of. It's sort of like Dorothy in *The Wizard Of Oz*. During the tornado that sent her to another world, she faced obstacles in that other world, but all the while, she had within her reach the power to click her heels together and get home. She didn't realize it until the Good Witch pointed it out to her. In the wake of a tragedy, divorce, death, disaster, flu, plague, pandemic or economic upheaval, if we shift our perspective and can see how well equipped we already were to survive, we can now thrive. We can experience a new appreciation for our strengths and ourselves.

There are passages that we go through in life that general society tells us to react with sadness, grief, fear, complete and utter defeat, anger, self-doubt, repeated self-flagellation, failure, harsh judgment or suicide. If one meets a difficult passage in life with the aforementioned emotional response, one might not make it through to the other side. Here's the thing: going through the wilderness can lead to the Promised Land. You may not even know what your Promised Land is or that you have one, but let's dare to hope there is something better than the squalor you're sitting in right now. It's that hope that will carry you through your darkest times. And maybe there is beauty in the squalor? Maybe you learn things about

GET YOUR BUTT OFF MY COUCH

yourself and meet people and become enlightened in a way that would have never happened without going through the wilderness. At least that's what happened to me.

    I've faced wildernesses in my life. I couldn't see the forest through the trees. The problems in my life had snowballed and it looked like the tundra on a cold winter day. I was getting divorced. I had veered off the false sense of security of the track system I was on with all my girlfriends. The track system I'm referring to is analogous to the track system set-up by L.A. Unified School System. In recent history, the Los Angeles Unified school system set up tracks to accommodate the vast student body. There were too many high school students so the school board put students on tracks so they all weren't in school at the same time, but that meant that one's school year drastically changed. If you were on the A track, you went to school between July-March. So if you were a senior that would mean you'd graduate from high school in March with your other classmates on that track. Your summer break would begin in the spring. Your life would have to adhere and morph to fit this new track that you were arbitrarily placed on. You'd have to miss out on a summer experience in July and August because the school board had chosen this new path for your life. There are life tracks in adulthood as well. If we're not careful to lay our own tracks, we end up living out our life on someone else's.

I was on the marriage and children track with many other friends. When I separated from my husband, three of my friends on the track were pregnant with their second babies. In fact, when I called my friend Chris to give her the news about my divorce, she shared with me the news of her pregnancy and before I could tell her about my separation, she told me that I needed to get started on getting pregnant to keep up with her because her first child and my son shared the same exact birthday. It feels safe and comfortable to be going through the same stages in life right alongside your friends. I was grateful for sharing the journey of motherhood with girlfriends. At that particular time in my life I was completely off of the track, but in a good way.

Back then I didn't think, *fantastic! Finally I'm off someone else's track.* Now I can begin to find my own way and live my own life. Un-yoking myself from my marriage was my first step. It was a gift, wrapped up in tears and pain, but still it was life affirming. Part of what impeded my ability to look forward and hope after my divorce was embedded in the pity and sadness that people: friends, family, and acquaintances expressed about the end of the marriage. When I told people I was getting divorced, I got the sad face look from everyone. The face is best described as a head-slant with turned down lip and sad eyes. This countenance projects their empathy, sympathy, pity and whatever else society or their mothers have trained them to think or feel about divorce or loss. Along with the sad head-slant face I always got a heartfelt, sometimes pained: I'm sorry. Then, the really sad part was I would catch their pity energy and internalize it. Pity doesn't exude compassion. Pity is judgmental. Pity makes you feel pathetic.

Yes, I had sadness about the end of my marriage. For me getting out of a relationship that is not working is like being fired from a job that wasn't the right fit. There's ambivalence because you need the job for money and being employed fits conventions of society. But being fired from a job that isn't right for you gives you freedom to go find something or someone who is right. You can stop pretending and trying to make things work in a situation that is irreparable. When my marriage ended, I felt utter freedom: a release. Like an aged Heavy Weight Champion of the World, I had been holding onto a title belt that no longer fit me. One of my attorneys told me that before his marriage ended he had many sleepless nights, but the first night of separation he finally slept like a baby. He was at peace.

When we release something that is not uplifting or affirming us there is peace. I felt that peace. Now admittedly after my separation and during the divorce process there was turmoil, but my turmoil was self-created because I chose to fight instead of just let go. In the state of California, when two parties divorce the court seeks to equally distribute financial assets regardless of gender, which meant I had to pay alimony. Just as the court said my ex was entitled to a portion of my paycheck, I felt entitled to all of it. Entitlement is an ugly thing. It doesn't leave room for gratitude. Entitlement is like a two-year old fighting another two-year old over a toy while screaming and yelling, "mine, mine, mine." Long before Columbus discovered America, the Native People lived communally. The land was not divvied up and sold. There were no mortgages, nor a housing collapse because Citibank or Freddie Mac didn't own the land. It belonged to all people. What's ironic is that our judicial system invokes this communal, tribal policy in divorce court. In a society that tells us to "get yours" where the individual is king this antithetical communal philosophy rules in cases of divorce; therefore, my adverse reaction to having to pay alimony made sense, but it was still ugly and toddler-like. I didn't have compassion for my ex-husband, but that made sense because I didn't have compassion for myself either. I was just plowing through life trying to maintain a stiff upper lip and only allowed myself minimal moments to feel my pain because I had to work and raise a child, which didn't leave room to love myself, or listen to my inner voice. Plus walking through pain takes courage and I didn't have that yet. Instead I listened to my ego.

My ego cost me a lot of money. I think in general egos are expensive. You have to dress them up and make them feel good. Egos have to buy fancy cars because they get jealous easily. My ego lined my divorce lawyers' pockets. My ego told me that I was entitled to keep all my money. It told me that my ex-husband shouldn't get alimony because he's an able-bodied man. Yes, I was willing to give him a certain amount of money that I had decided in my arbitrary life rules was what he deserved, but what I was giving him was not from my heart or out of generosity, but out of pity, anger, spite and fear. The Bible says to be a cheerful giver, but what I was proposing to give was not out of cheer. It was nowhere near cheer. It was fear that compelled me to hold on tight to my wallet. The fear, however, was masked by anger.

I acquiesced in the end realizing that I had no other choice, but to pay alimony. I even told my lawyers to let him have the list of material possessions he wanted like our wedding crystal and silver. I waved my white flag because I knew this was a battle I couldn't win and the material possessions were not a big deal to me. But to buoy my ego that didn't get her way, I decided to speak poorly of my ex. What I said about my ex-husband was seemingly haughty and bold and did not tip off the fear that was lurking just beneath the surface I told my mother and others that I would always make more money than my ex-husband. I had to devalue his worth to make myself feel better. The true roots of that statement were my feelings of unworthiness masked with pride. Those statements were my ego asserting itself into the situation. I was making statements of grandiosity, but what I really needed was a dose of humility and compassion. Who was I to say something like that? It was bad enough to think such thoughts about another person, but to utter them aloud, to believe in the power of my words and myself, was so ungodly and so mean-spirited, yet so forgivable. I am grateful for forgiveness. Those harsh words expressed more about my fear of my own economic failure than my ex-husband's earning potential. The irony of all this is in recent history I've had to humble myself and ask my ex-husband for money. I've had to ask him for money to pay for basics like food and gas and he's been generous enough to think of me and give me more money than I've asked for to help me, the mother of his child. Unlike me, he has been a cheerful giver.

My harsh words predicting my economic success over his came back to haunt me. My fear, which is inverted faith, came true. I haven't always made more money than my husband. In fact, recently I basically lost all of my money, but I found self-love. When I lost almost everything of material value, I really did gain more. What I didn't know about myself -- what I didn't learn during my divorce was that I based my self-worth in my economic and professional success--typical American dream stuff--which I've learned is all ego. Although I had to pay alimony and make some financial sacrifices while divorced, I still had a prestigious job, was a client of one of the most prominent and powerful talent agencies in the world and still had more than enough money coming in so I was able to lull myself into this false sense of security and rested my faith in my bank account and my ability to make it larger.

People who believed in my talent surrounded me. Later I would learn their belief was limited. I had people around me who had the nerve to say I was better than my ex-husband. How dare they say that? But at the time I did not refute their statements. What I had placed my hope and belief in wasn't anything stable. When it came down to it, I had put my faith and self-worth in business. It's easy to support someone when business is up, when the money is rolling in and when they're in the economic black. It's easy to believe in yourself when you have money and when people around you are telling you your future looks bright. The only future that these people are concerned about is your healthy, prosperous economic future from which they will get a percentage. Do not be deceived into believing that business people have any sort of real interest in your personal journey. Their only interest in you personally is when it conflicts or impedes your ability to make money or reach professional or economic milestones they've set out for you, which may or may not be the milestones you're really destined for. Do you see the pattern here? Like the life track that I was on with my girlfriends when I was married and they were all having their second babies, but I was getting divorced,

I had linked myself with a "team" which is code for agents, managers, and professional mentors etc., who also put me on a track because they saw my professional future a certain way. Their point of view is based on their own conscious or sub-conscious biases, beliefs, their own professional agendas, competition, monthly quotas, business agendas, personal taste, connections etc. So for me to try to fulfill their track would be like me trying to fulfill someone else's dreams and life path. This is where I betrayed myself in life again. First I betrayed myself in my marriage and in other romantic relationships by not listening to my inner voice, then I did it again in business to try to please others so they'd like me and keep hiring me and continue to get me work. I wanted to please "my team" and do what was expected of me and make lots of money. I felt like a racehorse they were sponsoring and when racehorses don't win they get sent out to pasture.

People pleasing and the need for other's approval is a cancer and the root causes of that cancer are fear and a lack of self-worth. It has been said that men do what they want and women do as they're told. I think our society does socialize females to be good little girls and being good means being accommodating and pleasing. I'm not blaming society or anyone for my life choices, but understanding how I have been socialized helps me understand my choices. When we go through our lives needing approval from others we must understand that other's approval as I stated before has to do with their specific point of view, their agendas, biases, and desires. When we seek the approval of others we're in effect fulfilling their wants, dreams, and agendas for our lives. When you go through life fulfilling someone else's dreams and agendas that's like wearing someone else's underpants. So the next time you think you need someone else's approval about your choice for a career, a mate, clothing, food or even which direction you're driving, ask yourself if you'd wear their underpants.

I am a recovering people pleaser. My people pleasing disorder has only caused me heartache, pain and an empty bank account, but as I walked through all of that it has led to my recovery and freedom from my disease to please. Some people wait until their forties and fifties or never to stop giving a shit about what other people think, or trying to please others. Do yourself a favor and stop giving a shit today.

The first root cause of the people pleasing/approval disorder is low self-worth. Although I have achieved a lot in my career, I never relished in or appreciated or even thought much of those achievements because I was always striving to achieve more. I didn't think I was enough because my self-worth was based on my success, approval and achievements. I felt like I needed to achieve more and more and more to actually have value and worth. Even when the executive producer of *Will & Grace* told me that Creative Artists Agency a.k.a. CAA was lucky to have me as a client, I didn't quite feel that or absorb it or believe it. I've always been one to subdue compliments. If you look for your self-worth outside of yourself whether in society, your parents, your priest, any human being, success or achievements, you'll end up self-destructing because those things are always changing.

Success and achievement were my Achilles' heel. I made an idol out of success and any idol other than God will always let you down. I come from a family of high achievers so in some ways I thought success was my birthright. Members of my family have succeeded in sports at the highest level. My father is a Hall Of Fame Football Player. When I was in third grade there was a local television special about my dad. I didn't even know it was going to be airing until my third grade teacher told me about it because my dad is not ego-driven and it really wasn't a big deal in our house. The sports gene doesn't begin and end with my dad. My brother was awarded an athletic scholarship to play baseball at San Diego State. He's always been adept at all sports. Even though I would practice tennis for hours, my brother, who barely played, could pick up a racquet and launch a backhand, forehand or serve with precision, spin and speed. My cousin, Stephanie Hightower, was an outstanding track and field star and a member of the ill-fated 1980 Olympic team. My aunt is an accomplished opera singer who has performed on Broadway, at the Metropolitan

GET YOUR BUTT OFF MY COUCH

Opera and internationally. My mom was a successful business owner.

My dad has always been my biggest supporter and never made me feel like I wasn't enough. Both of my parents are extremely hard working and humble. My dad has always encouraged me to be an individualist and follow my dreams. Despite the message I got from him, pride and my ego needed recognition. My ego bought into what society tells us about our worth. We are conditioned as a society to believe that our worth is in our achievements and success rather than we are all worthy because we're singular creations of almighty God.

Before I got this revelation, I was still driven by ego, success and the need to be recognized. I inherited the familial athletic gene, but I suffered a debilitating knee injury early into my gymnastics career. I had to quit the sport that I loved and then I found the theater, also known as an oasis for the ego. I recall my mom asking me when I was about twelve what I wanted to be when I grew up and I told her: an actress. She told me she was spending a lot of money on a private school and it wasn't for me to become an actress. She wanted me to be something like a lawyer or a judge. I never became an actress or a lawyer or a judge, but in some ways I always felt like my pursuits were not lauded enough or understood. Yet, my parents gave me the space and education to pursue my dreams.

My choice to pursue the arts was not met with the same

understanding, enthusiasm and approval from my mid-western family and friends, who didn't really understand entertainment as well as sports. This fueled my drive for success even more. In some ways, I needed to prove to them and others that this wasn't just a pipe dream. Back in Ohio we didn't even know that people were paid to write Fonzie's lines on *Happy Days*. My friends and family told me I watched too much TV and that was never going to get me anywhere. I was pursuing a career that was completely foreign to my family and friends, which meant that I had to do it big so everyone could see and know that I was a success. The irony is that even when I was doing it big on a prime time hit network show, I couldn't feel and absorb my accomplishment. I wrote episodes of *Will & Grace* that millions of people watched, but it simply wasn't enough.

Unlike other endeavors, success and achievement seemed like something within my grasp. I was naïve enough to believe that if I worked hard enough and sacrificed everything, including having a life, that success was attainable, but my drive was also fueled by fear: the fear that I could not succeed in anything else. I was also searching for some sort of identity outside of myself, which was an enormous misstep, especially in the arts when our best work comes from within our hearts. My pursuit of the arts was my means to success, identity and people pleasing. There's nothing better than applause from a live audience that communicates that they like me.

Success is like a drug habit that can never be quenched. There's always another level of success to reach. The high from one success is short-lived because you're looking for the next level. I had, as Dr. Kevin Leman described in his book *The New Birth Order Book,* a perfectionist personality. "This kind of personality walks around holding up what I call the high-jump bar of life. She is always raising the bar a little higher and is a master at defeating herself at every turn." In my success addiction there wasn't room for gratitude or even acknowledgment of the success that I had reached. I never celebrated myself really because it was never enough. I never took time to really give thanks or be in the moment and enjoy and honor my achievements. Some people may have looked at my career and assumed I was pursuing my dreams, but I allowed my dreams to be hijacked. Because I was still trying to please others and I had great fear of failure, of not being good enough, of disapproval, my dreams got hijacked and I permitted the jacking.

When I first began to write, I wrote from my heart and that is what drove me, but that's not always what television writing is about. Typical writing on a television sit-com involves people shouting joke pitches at a showrunner like they are bidding on an antique at auction and then hoping the showrunner accepts their bid. It can be fast, dirty and frenzied in writers' rooms. It can also be a lot of fun. I've been in writers' rooms dominated by fear where people were being fired, leadership was not strong and actors were unhappy. Those types of rooms can be chaotic and draining. I've been in rooms dominated by peace and joy where creativity can flourish and writing is fantastically fun and you feel like you're making harmonious music with like-minded musicians. You're living the dream.

You're also getting paid a tremendous amount of money to live your dream or your nightmare. The former scenario of the room dominated by fear is one of oppression, but for some the money and fame associated with show business can be so tempting that it lures you away from the real reason you wanted to write in the first place and enables you to stay in a place that can be oppressive.

The truth is Hollywood will hijack your dreams if you let it. Just as we allow ourselves to do things in relationships and go places that aren't true to who we are, we can do the same in business. Because I was on a track and had allowed other people to hijack my dream, I wasn't true to myself or my art, which was only detrimental to me and extremely ironic since at age eighteen I chose the Shakespearean quote: "This above all to thine own self be true," to be printed on my yearbook page. Here is one instance in which I allowed my dreams to be commandeered.

I recall writing a pilot for NBC. I had received notes from the producers, the studio and the network on my script. Because

I was trying to please everyone, I attempted to address all of the notes. I was writing what people told me to write instead of being true to my original vision. In some ways, I was like a woman trying to conform my hair, body and clothing to some pop-culture, media, societal standard of beauty. I was in effect one of those plastic surgery junkies trying to make myself into the perfect Barbie. If a man wants a Barbie, he should go to Toys-R-Us. If he wants a real woman with cellulite, morning breath and a good sense of humor, he should open his eyes to see those precious gems all around him. And if those executives wanted my true vision for the script I created, then they needed to let me be me. The problem was I listened to their voices, like women who look at pop-culture images and try to emulate them. I doubted my own beauty, worth and creativity.

Unlike the unrelenting battle we wage against saddlebags and gray hair, I relented with my unique script that had lost its individuality while trying to conform to what others wanted it to be. I lost my fervor for the script because I was listening to too many voices and couldn't hear my own anymore. My goal was to please others so they'd promote me and make my pilot into a TV series rather than to stay true to my artistic vision. I was afraid that if I didn't write what they wanted me to write, they wouldn't promote me, or make my pilot, or work with me again. At some point during this ridiculous process, one of the executives was brave enough to say that, "We've given you too many notes at this point. Why don't you go back and try to remember what inspired you to write this in the first place?" I remember thinking: what inspired me to write this in the first place was the check had cleared. I had allowed money to hijack my dream. I was no longer writing from my heart, but from my fearful pocketbook. A pocketbook that feared scarcity and was willing to sell out to ensure it would always be full, but that was stupid. Here's what happened: I wrote some version of what I thought they wanted me to write. I turned in the script and NBC rejected it. They paid me, but they didn't make the pilot. The studio, which had originally hired me to write the script, did not hire me again. So there I was trying to please all of these people because I wanted their approval and for them to produce my pilot; I wanted them to continue to fill up my pocketbook, but I didn't get any of that. On top of all of that I wasn't true to my art or myself.

I've always admired girls with blue hair because they have the guts to be who they are. Convention be damned. Don't be the good girl, be the girl with the blue hair. Live your life. Be like Sia and do an interpretive dance like she does in the video for the song "Chandelier." She's a grown woman in her Danskins who is unafraid to express herself. When we compromise who we are whether it's in business or in love we end up with big, fat, losers on our couch because compromise bleeds into every aspect of life. It becomes second nature because we stop believing we can ever get what we want or do what we really want to do so we settle for what crosses our path or what others tell us we should want or are willing to give us. When we stop listening to our own voices it becomes easier to listen to others and let them speak for you. Find your voice and then scream from the mountaintops. Don't end up living a life or doing a job or trying to love a man because you think that's what you're supposed to do or because it will make other people happy or because it won't rock anybody's boat. What about your boat? That's the one that counts.

There were times in my career when I stopped to ask people on my team what am I doing and what is this leading to, but as soon as I would question it, money would get in the way and my questions would disappear.

I measure success in my work now when I write from my heart. Eleanor Roosevelt said, "Do what you feel in your heart to be right--for you'll be criticized anyway." It is the work that I've truly written from my heart, unfettered by network notes, by other's opinions, by any voice other than the one screaming from within--it is that work--heart work--that has been well received. That work has garnered attention, accolades and even monetary success. When I work from my heart, I am being true to myself.

The belief that quieted the doubt, fear, the need to please wasn't brought on by great success. Believe it or not, it was born out of what some would describe as failure, but I describe as a gift. What is true for me now is that success is not who I am. If I'm successful, it is because God has given me talent and opened doors for me to flourish. In order to get off of the success addiction I had to die to my pride and ego and recognize God. My success masked a false sense of control I thought I had over my life. And control is this ridiculous man-made idea that tries to help us make sense of life. So we make plans, we follow rules, we do what others have done or what others expect or want us to do or what society compels us to do. We try all these things to control our piece of this world so that our life turns out the way we want it to, but the cold hard truth that shatters this ridiculous notion of control is that we're all just on some planet that's floating in outer space and nobody really knows anything for sure. So now I just listen to the voice inside my heart and my gut. That is my Spirit. If you don't believe that there is a God and you are somehow controlling everything, then good luck. For me, I know that it's with God that all things are possible. So I give God the glory, the gratitude and accept the gifts He's given me. God does surprising miraculous things in our lives every day, but sadly we don't take the time to acknowledge, honor or show gratitude for his everyday miracles. Sometimes we even think they are of our doing. We constantly expect more, or feel as if we have not done enough. We fear the future rather than greet it with faith and expectancy. I would fear the future too if I thought I was somehow in charge of what was to come, but I greet the future with faith and expectancy that God gives good and perfect gifts and orders my steps. I pray His will over my life and not my own and certainly not other peoples.

As for me, it matters very little how I might be evaluated by you or by any human authority. I don't even trust my own judgment on this point. My conscience is clear, but that doesn't prove I'm right. It is the Lord himself who will examine me and decide. 1Corninthians 4:3-4

Here is how I got off the success/achievement hamster wheel and to the aforementioned truths. I am still very much a work in progress. It is with prayer and reading scripture and fellowship and love that I am able to walk the walk as they say with many missteps along the way. I got divorced and still had worldly romantic hope because society instills romantic hope in us at birth from Disney and fairy-lies, to every Meg Ryan, Kate Hudson, Jennifer Lopez starring romantic-comedy. Society brands us with a romantic dream so strong that even when I'm eighty years old in the retirement village, I may still believe that dream lives.

The other side of this is that people easily tell us to give up on our other dreams. Give up on the dream of being in the NBA, or winning an Academy Award, or marrying George Clooney. Clooney is not available now, but the self-professed life-long bachelor did make Amaal's dream come true. So keep dreaming girls, not for Amaal's man, for someone else. Society has named wistful, foolish dreams: pipe dreams. As defined by Dictionary.com, pipe dreams are visions as a result of taking opiates. Instead, I like to call these dreams: heart dreams. They are born in your heart. It's our heads that talk us out of these dreams. At age twelve my son, like a lot of kids, has NBA aspirations and has been told by more people (a lot of them annoying little kids on the playground) that he'll never be in the NBA. Everything is possible. In Luke 1 verse 37: "For with God nothing shall be impossible." Even if you don't believe in God or the Bible it's nice to believe in a positive message rather than a negative one. If we dare to believe this verse and apply it to our lives, we make room for impossibility and shut down negative voices.

The future is not guaranteed. Your story is still being written; therefore, don't let people talk you out of the dream born in your heart because they don't know how your story is going to end. In the 2015 Superbowl, Seahawks rookie Chris Matthews, who just signed with the team, made an outstanding play after play in the first half of the game. Matthews was cut from the Cleveland Browns in 2011 and had basically given up on football. A couple of months before the 2015 Superbowl, Matthews was working at Foot Locker. In fact when they called to ask him to fly to Seattle for a try-out, Matthews told them he didn't know if he could make it because he didn't get off of work until 9pm. Matthews made the try-out *and* the team and history in the Superbowl.

Jim Morris had dreams of becoming a major league baseball pitcher. He was drafted to the Milwaukee Brewers, but suffered shoulder injuries that ended his career. Many years later at age thirty-five years old with a wife and three children, Morris, who was a high school science teacher, tried out for the Tampa Bay Devil Rays. He pitched in the major leagues and at thirty-five was named the oldest rookie in MLB in forty years. Disney made a film, *The Rookie*, starring Dennis Quaid about his story. Many Hollywood actors like Terri Hatcher and John Travolta have gone years or decades in between notable roles. People, colleagues, critics have prematurely called time of death on their careers before their amazing second acts.

We hold these false beliefs that we're too old, or it's too late or we've missed our window of opportunity we were going to climb through or the boat that was going to help us get to the place where we can attain our dreams. Who invented that bullshit about being too old and missing the boat or window of opportunity? Who closed that window of opportunity? Who says it's too late or it's never going to happen? Unless that person is God, then he or she has no business forecasting the future. I believe that it's the negative voices in our heads that inhibit us. We are our biggest obstacles. Yes, you may come across people who tell you, you're too old, but they are those negative talkers whom we must block out at all costs. Unless you're at port and you see the boat sailing off without you, you have not missed the boat of life. It's not too late for you to reach your goals, go after your dreams, and as Henry David Thoreau says, "live the life you've imagined." Or, re-imagine a new life. Please just don't live the life others have imagined for you. People talk themselves out of their dreams in order to avoid the pain of never reaching them. Yet that compounds the pain. There is pain in a dream deferred. There is also pain in self-doubt and the unspeakable pain of those who never even try and simply give up on their dreams altogether. Langston Hughes said, "Hold fast to your dreams, for if dreams die life is a broken winged bird that cannot fly."

Society and people, even loved ones, unwittingly conspire to kill our dreams. Sometimes dreams are murdered as soon as we muster up the courage to speak them, or as soon as we're on the precipice of achieving them. Our dreams get killed for a great number of reasons, but the main reason is that other people do not have the ability to believe. Sometimes their disbelief is wrapped up in their lack of belief in themselves or in anything unseen. These people lack faith of all kinds. These are same people who need to see it to believe it and even when they see it, they don't believe it will last. These are negative thinkers, feelers and beings. They are worse than dream hijackers because they don't even let you dare to dream. They are unbelievers. If you let their negative talk get into your head, you'll become one of them. Beware of anyone who dares to tell you that something will never happen. It's important to bless them, forgive them for their unbelief, ignore their negative talk and continue on your life path. I've encountered these high-level negative talkers. They have elevated their negativity game to the highest level and have the audacity to actually say out loud that something will never happen. Here are how a couple of those encounters have gone. I started school at Ithaca College in New York. I knew as a freshman that I wanted to transfer to the University Of Southern California and into their school of Cinema-Television. While at Ithaca I made the Dean's List. As I prepared my application for USC, I needed recommendation letters from professors. I was getting an A in one of my film classes and I asked that professor if he'd write me a letter of recommendation. He agreed to do it, but to my surprise, he matter-of-factly told me that I'd never get into USC School of Cinema because they are very elite and I simply don't have what it takes to get into that school. He said he'd write me the letter anyway. I was aghast and hurt. At nineteen years old I didn't yet possess the wherewithal to tell him off. He was still my professor, but I didn't agree with him. I let him write the letter and when he gave it to me in the sealed envelope, I thanked him and then I disposed of it.

I asked another professor who was more than willing to write a letter of recommendation and wished me all the best. I was admitted to USC School of Cinema Television and graduated from there. I now teach writing classes at USC School of Cinematic Arts.

Another instance of a negative talker occurred when my son was an infant. He had a tear duct problem. His left eye was constantly tearing and our pediatrician told us to see a specialist who could surgically correct it. My now ex-husband took our son to this doctor because I was working. After the appointment, my ex-husband told me that the doctor scheduled a surgery date for our son. I wasn't ready to have my baby go under the knife. I called to talk to the doctor about the procedure and to see if anything could be done non-surgically, or could he grow out of this. The arrogant doctor told me that this problem would never correct itself and surgery was the only way. I told the doctor that I needed time to think about this and pray about it. To which he responded that I could pray if I wanted, but nothing was going to change. This would never go away and he had many people waiting to have this surgery so I needed to decide right now or else he'd gladly give our surgery date to someone else. I told him that I'd like to pray about it and he could give the surgery date to someone else and I'd get back to him. Well, I prayed about my son's eye. I enlisted others to pray for his healing and my son never got that surgery because his eye healed. The chronic tears from his left eye stopped after a few months. So "never" doesn't hold up.

I believe it is easier to tell someone no than to say yes. When you say yes, that usually means you have to do some work after that yes. You have to help them in some way because you have said yes. No is a conversation ender and also means you don't have to lift a finger because you've ended the discussion by saying no. I don't understand where these never people get off forecasting absolutes into anyone's future. How can one proclaim such an edict as *never* over someone's life unless they have delusions of grandeur? Even world-renowned surgeons leave room for healing miracles and God.

There is one other kind of negative talker we must beware of. They are crafty in their negativity because they try to disguise it in espousing words of faith and belief in you. Has anyone ever said to you, "I believe in you. You're going to make it. You're going to get that job or marry that man, or lose that weight, or win that race, or get that promotion, or get that house, or graduate, <u>but</u> if you don't you need to make a plan for what you'll do when that doesn't happen?" BUT. The *but* negates all of the preceding positive affirmations. The *but* communicates that I really don't believe in you and I fear the worst. The *but* tells you to prepare for your dreams and goals NOT to come true because all the stuff I said before the but was bullshit. It tells you to prepare for failure. Sometimes they even have you make a failure plan instead of a success celebration. How can one even make a wholehearted attempt at achieving anything when the person who is supposed to be in your corner is preparing you to fail? Get that anti-cheerleader off of your sidelines in life. Bless them and send them on their way. Replace them with positivity, belief and faith.

We all need a positive reward system in our lives. Recently I discovered how miraculous positive rewards are. Our son was not doing his homework. His father and I were at our wit's end. We'd punish him for not finishing something, but a child therapist we saw gave us the sage advice to try a reward system. We were inspiring our son NOT to try because we had taken away his hope. He knew that if he did not do what was expected he'd get something taken away, but we were putting a negative upon a negative. He already viewed homework as a negative endeavor so we were only going to punish him with another negative rather than reward him with something positive and turn homework into a positive experience. Rather than punish him for not doing his homework, we set up a great reward system to inspire him to complete his work. Suddenly things changed. He had hope that if he did his homework he'd get some positive reinforcement. It worked. He looks forward (not all of the time) to doing his homework because he knows his hard work will be rewarded. We removed the negativity and turned it positive.

We all have the capacity to do that with every situation in life even the ones that are defined by society as awful or terrible. We move through passages and seasons in life to get us to the next place. We can grow from each season: the difficult trials and the joyous parties. Don't let a negative spin or someone's negative words rob you of pursuing your purpose and living your life. Like Miss Janet Jackson and the soap opera says: "you've got one life to live."

Negative, never and but people are not necessarily malevolent. In fact, they probably mean well. Their unbelief has to do with their personal journey, not yours, and their appropriation of negative societal and cultural beliefs. Often, their unbelief has to do with fear. Fear of failure. Fear of faith. Fear of hope.

There is no fear in love. But perfect love drives out fear because fear has to do with punishment. The one who fears is not made perfect in love. 1John 4:18

CHAPTER FOURTEEN

Afraid to Hope

Hope is a scary endeavor. You have to be brave to have hope because sometimes we hope for things, but then we don't get them and our hope is crushed. In order not to feel the crushing blow again of lost hope, we resign from hoping altogether. Instead, to protect our fragile human state and toughen up, we believe in the negative. We assume the worst will happen so that if the best happens we're happily surprised. When we do that we call negativity into action. Six months into dating a boyfriend, we had a negative conversation about our relationship. I'd characterize it as negative because he was forecasting negativity into our future. He believed that things would not work out between us because he was in a transition in his life and he was planning on moving out of state and in his projection he did not see how we could maintain a connection. He was trying to be pragmatic and spare us both pain and disappointment. Somehow within that conversation I had what our president has called: the audacity of hope. I dared to believe that the best was yet to come instead of the worst. I told him he was putting out fires that didn't exist. He was truly speaking negativity into a situation that wasn't negative. We were two fragile human beings trying to make it in this big, bad world, who had been fortunate enough to find each other under weird circumstances and make a connection, but perhaps to stave off future pain that he was predicting, he wanted to curtail this romantic endeavor before the pain got unbearable. But as the saying goes *we're better off having loved than never loved at all*. The experience of the relationship we shared was enriching in all aspects of my life for nearly four years. If one wakes up every morning without daring to hope that the best is yet to come, then what is life, but drudgery through the muck of mere existence. That is not living.

Hope is something I work at everyday. I didn't really become hopeful until I had experienced great loss, which seems incongruous, but in facing a big fear is where I gained hope. I first had to understand the fear more to see where my hope had died and fear had taken over.

Before I was on staff at *Will & Grace*, I was hired to write a freelance episode of the Emmy-award winning series. When I told my mom about the job, her reception wasn't joyous. It was fearful. When I told her my good news, her reaction was, "What if they don't like what you write? Will you still get paid?" That's fear. What I told her was, "They are going to love it." I don't believe her intention was to instill fear in me, but that's exactly what it did. She was genuinely concerned about my well-being, but her question hurt and caused fear to fester and grow. Her question did not feel supportive and it stuck with me for years. In fact, that incident occurred over a decade ago yet as I write this today I can recount the details of that moment as if it were happening now. She had just entered my apartment. This brief exchange took place practically in the doorway because I wanted to greet my mom with my good news as she entered my home. As I delivered my news, I got served with a body blow by my mother's comment. Though my retort was strong and positive somewhere within me, even though I exuded confidence, was fear and her comment exacerbated it. Fear is like a tapeworm that seeks to devour its host. It only needs a little bit of nourishment to continue its demise.

Fear is not necessarily malicious. It's just scared to death. Fear that has been cultivated and fed is like overgrown vines of ivy that wind around and form a stranglehold on your life until the breath has been choked out of you. Fear is what keeps big, fat, losers on our couches; fear that we can't do any better than this triflin' loser on my couch; fear of an empty couch, or an empty, lonely life, fear of standing up for yourself to evict him from the couch; fear of facing reality and yourself and why you'd allow a big, fat, loser on your couch in the first place. Fear is a man-made lie that if you choose to believe it and feed it, it will keep you stuck and far from your dreams and an abundant life. Hope is a spiritual life force that carries us to our destiny with joy and thanksgiving. Feed hope.

Years into my career as a professional screenwriter, I had concluded a second development deal with HBO. The deal did not end as I had hoped. As a television writer when you're paid to write a pilot script, the ending you hope for after you've written the script is that the network will actually shoot your pilot and then put it on the air. That did not happen. I called my mom to tell her the news and her reaction was that I should just get a regular job at a corporation. After this one project did not work out her answer was to quit the business altogether. Again that was not wishing me any ill will, but her words were spoken out of fear. By the way, this isn't one of those "blame everything on your mother books." My mom's belief, desires, fears and dreams for her children probably resemble that of most American mothers. She has always wanted the best for me. She grew up in the 50's and 60's when people worked at big corporations. They worked for a lifetime at one company and retired well, but she was giving me this advice in 2010 when America's corporate landscape had vastly changed and no one could count on anything from corporate America except an empty 401K, a tax payer subsidized bail out and a pink slip. I also had no experience working in corporate America. Her advice came from her specific POV, her history, her agenda and her fears. Once again it fed my fear. In some ways, I believed I appropriated her fear of lack. My mom grew up poor. She was blessed and grateful that she and my dad could give my brother and me everything monetarily and that we never had to experience the economic worries and fears she had experienced in her youth. Society conditions us into believing that success and money are everything. But at that moment in my life, when my project had failed and money was becoming scarce, I had neither, thus I had nothing and in effect, I was nothing.

This belief about money and success was also tied to the decadent 80's, also known as my formative years. I was raised in an affluent suburb of Cleveland, Ohio. I went to an expensive private school. I didn't know what financial aid was until I got to college and friends had to do work-study. I hadn't even considered the cost of college when I applied. My parents weren't completely indulgent. They didn't buy me a car for the sweet sixteen, but I did get to drive one of my parents' cars. My choices were my mom's Audi 5000 or my dad's convertible red Mercedes Benz. What I lacked from this life of affluence was perspective. Everything I knew to be of importance in life was wrapped up in success whether that was in school, sports or business and that's where I found my self-worth. I wasn't boastful or materialistic. In fact, I just took it for granted that I could buy a pair of Guess jeans whenever I wanted. I trusted that every Spring Break would be spent someplace like the Bahamas or Bermuda. Because my way of life was never challenged and seemed to be a constant, my value and identity seemed to be tied to that way of life.

After my mom proposed that I get a job at a corporation, I tried to do what I had been doing but what had not really been working and get back on this track/path that others had laid out for me, instead of making my own track. I didn't have enough faith in myself yet. I had fear. The only thing I chose to hang onto was my faith in a process that had previously worked. It seemed like the old way was kind of working again. At the end of 2010, I was approached by a successful Hollywood movie producer to come up with a pitch for a movie about a cruise. When I was first told about the project, I had some initial misgivings. The little voice inside of me said this job isn't for you, but I was desperate. I needed a job. The holidays were approaching and Hollywood basically shuts down between Thanksgiving and the New Year so I thought this may be my only shot at finding work before the holidays. Fear fueled my decision to go after this job.

Now Hollywood doesn't work like the real world where you go to your job, do work and are paid your wages at the end of the week. Hollywood, and especially the feature film business, works backwards. Unless one is in the elite group of Hollywood A-listers who are offered jobs, one has an elaborate audition process. As a writer, actor and director, in order to get hired to write, act or direct a film one must prove that they are the best candidate for the job. This proving process goes way beyond wowing someone in an interview and sending a spectacular thank you note. As a writer who is being considered to write a movie, one must come up with all of the characters and the entire plot of the movie and pitch it to a series of executives before one gets the job. Even if the prospective writer does all of that work, there is no guarantee that he or she will get the job, nor is there any money upfront for all that work. That writer is also competing with several other writers, but even if one is the only writer who is pitching her idea to the movie studio, there is still no guarantee that the studio will buy the pitch. If the studio doesn't buy it, there's no paycheck at the end of that long process; therefore you've been working for free. Yes, for free for weeks or months. I know what you're thinking: wasn't slavery abolished in 1865? Tell that to Hollywood. Actors too can go through weeks and months of auditions and testing and still not get the job. Getting close to being hired doesn't pay the light bill.

So there I was in 2010, desperately seeking a paycheck and because this system of working for free and pitching my idea and then getting hired had worked for me many times in the past, I didn't have the logical reservations of working for free. I did have other reservations. Intuitively, there was something off about this prospective job, but I couldn't pinpoint it. I decided to quell that voice and make a deal with myself. If I could come up with a take for the movie about a cruise, then I'd move forward and pitch the project, but if I couldn't come up with an idea, then my intuition was right and this job is not for me. Because I'm a creative person, I was able to come up with an idea for the movie. I pitched it to the producer and he loved it. I was brought in after the first of the year to pitch to the studio and they bought it. So I had a contract and a job... sort of. There was one missing piece to my contract. The studio was negotiating to close a rights deal with the creator of the cruise. My contract was predicated on their closing that rights deal, but I was assured the deal would be closed. In the meantime, the actual cruise was taking place and the studio paid for a friend and me to take the cruise, but because the rights deal wasn't closed the studio waited until the last minute to buy my plane ticket to the port. There were so many difficulties and communication issues involving this trip that I wasn't even sure I would get to go on the cruise. My intuition continued to tell me that this was not going to work out and this wasn't the job for me, but I continued to deny that voice because I was living in fear of lack and I needed this job and this paycheck. I wasn't trusting in God or my inner voice that I believe is spirit generated. I put my trust in a pretty shitty contract that protected the big movie studio not me. I was trusting in the process and in the business. "Don't put your hope in material things" is what just about everyone says from the Dali Lama to the people in the Bible, including God, to the guy standing at the freeway underpass holding a sign that reads, "Don't put your hope in material things." Really if you think about it, the only security you can count on when you have a lot of money is that you'll never have to walk around looking like a back woods, Butcher Holler hillbilly without a front tooth. Having money will always enable you to afford good dental care and never having to worry about going through life with jacked up teeth. I did have dental, but I had put my hope, security and trust in my career. I was a fool. My reward was fool's gold, which is worthless.

After spending months working out an entire plot for a movie, all the characters, their back story, jokes, even some dialogue and the beginning, middle and ending of an entire movie that I had pitched and pitched again, I got a trip on a cruise. It wasn't a vacation. I was full of anxiety the entire time. I was using the computers on the ship to make contact with my agent and others back in Hollywood because I knew I needed a real writing job with a paycheck at the end of the week. When I returned from the cruise, the rights deal still wasn't closed, but I was asked to write an outline for the movie. I was reluctant because I knew that the studio didn't have to pay me anything until they closed the rights deal with the creator of the cruise. My intuition and spirit were screaming at me not to write this outline, but again I felt pressure and fear. I wanted to play ball. I wanted to be agreeable--people please. So I wrote the outline. Contractually, I would have been paid $25k for that outline. I say would have because the rights deal never closed and I was never paid anything for all the work that I did. I spent six months off and on working on this project and in the end I didn't make a dime. I didn't even win anything at the casino on the cruise ship.

 I learned an expensive lesson from this experience. I will always listen to my spirit and my intuition. I'll do an Olivia Pope gut check and trust that. My inner voice that I call spirit was basically screaming to me that my life was on fire, but I ignored it until I was burned and I couldn't deny it. That voice was sounding an alarm even on the cruise. I couldn't enjoy frolicking on the beach in Grand Cayman because my spirit was telling me that this deal is effed up and you've been working for free for six months and you're still not going to get paid. Some of you may be saying I didn't get totally screwed because I got to go on a free cruise. Well how many of you would forgo a year's pay for a weeklong cruise?

 I made a decision to pitch the project, go on the cruise and sign off on a pretty shitty contract all out of fear. I take full responsibility. My belief and trust were in the wrong place. There was a greater purpose to the cruise because I learned invaluable lessons. I came to a better understanding about how fear ruled my life and I made a conscious choice to stop making decisions based on fear. I also met some wonderful people on the cruise who have become dear friends and remain in my life. Above all else, I learned to value myself for who I am, not because of how much money is in my bank account, but because I am God's child.

While I also believe in the audacity of hope that our president Barack Obama so eloquently wrote about, I also believe in the audacity of humility. Real humility that isn't put-upon like when a shoe-in actor wins an Academy Award and tries to give a speech that doesn't seem rehearsed. I am no better than anyone else. Humility builds gratitude. Humility is the antithesis to entitlement. True humility reserves no judgment. To sit in judgment means that we know better. Who am I to say I know better or I know all things, or I can forecast the future, or I know what God intended for this seemingly bad situation in my life? The financial valley of my life seemed like a terrible situation, but God used it for good. I grew in faith, in compassion and in humility.

During my financial/career valley I got so many unsolicited words of advice, wisdom, thoughts, ideas about what I should do with my future, names of contacts with whom people had already contacted on my behalf without asking me, life plans that people had devised for me and I would have traded all of it for a hug and a prayer. Everyone's unsolicited, yet well-meaning advice benefitted him or her more than it did me. All the "You should" do this--to the, "You must do this"-- I even got, "I demand you to do this"-- made me feel like an elderly grandmother who others had deemed incapable of making decisions, or driving, or even choosing when she goes to the bathroom. I wish I had it in me then as soon as someone spoke their opinion into my life to tell them to shut the front door. I didn't get here because I made bad decisions about my finances. I didn't get here because I bought a yacht on a six-figure income. I didn't get here because I lived above my means. Yes, I do shop at Whole Foods, but I also shop at TJ Maxx so it all balances out. I got here because life is full of ups and downs. I'm here because none of us is guaranteed a bright and prosperous future without trouble. I'm here because this is part of my journey. I'm here because I have lessons to learn and places to grow.

The secret solution to get myself out of this valley was simply belief. To get to a place of belief requires a lot of de-programming. We basically have to throw out all the ideas that society, friends, family, business colleagues and strangers have instilled in us about value and understand that our true value is derived from within and not from outside accomplishments that people value. God loved us before we became what our résumés say we are. When those accomplishments fall away, we don't depreciate in value. As creations of God, our value is intrinsic.

CHAPTER FIFTEEN

Feelings Whoa, Whoa, Whoa Feelings...

Dr. Elaine Aron wrote a lovely book full of insight and wisdom entitled *The Highly Sensitive Person*. I only wish she had written it before I was born and hand delivered it to my parents. I am an artist and have always been sensitive and emotional. I was often accused of being too sensitive and too emotional and my parents meant emotional and sensitive in the pejorative sense. Like most teenagers, I felt like my angst was misunderstood. I know my parents did their best. I can only imagine that raising a teenager is something akin to managing a psychiatric fast food restaurant where the employees and patrons are teetering on the edge of stability. Parenting is not a business for the faint of heart and I honor my folks for completing their mission. They raised an artist. Art is all emotion and feeling. I grew up in a place where I felt like a misunderstood artist during a time when our society valued left-brains and I'm all right brain. Sadly, I missed the previous two decades, the 60's and 70's where it was all about feelings. In the 80's, and especially in the Midwest real feelings were suffocated with Denise Huxtable-like shoulder pads and money. So like many other teenagers and mid-westerners, I internalized my feelings while others expressed their pain as self-loathing or numbed it with fast food or other pain numbing devices.

We're a society that is pain phobic. We're afraid to feel emotional pain and trauma. We're afraid to feel the pain of disappointments, failures, divorces, break-ups, job loss, and death. We're essentially afraid of life because with life there are disappointments and loss. So we try to live life the safest way by avoiding pain, but pain is unavoidable. Then if we feel pain, we attempt to numb it with drugs, alcohol, food, sex or television. Pain is a way our lives speak to us. If you recall the Oprah story from an earlier chapter that fateful day my dear friend Kate's husband was watching porn and prevented the VCR from taping *Oprah* exposed a pain that she was trying to ignore with escaping to Oprah-land: the land of favorite things episodes and celebrity interviews. Truth be told, she wasn't really interested in getting real with Dr. Phil because she couldn't deal with the real pain of her life.

Pain is a wake up call. We need to feel it, walk through it, process it and learn from it. Even if we numb the pain out temporarily, it will come back to chase us. Even if we think we excise the pain by getting rid of what we think is the cause whether that be a husband, a boyfriend or a job, if we haven't dealt with the root of that pain, it will show up again in our lives. It may take on a different form, or the same. You may leave one man for another who looks completely different on the outside, but once you're in the relationship you feel the same pain. There's no easy escape from life's pain. And if we allow ourselves to feel it, we can get to a place of healing.

I've tried living the safe, pain free life route for years, but those conscious pain-avoidance choices have brought me the most pain because in making the "safe choice," I've hurt myself the most. I chose to marry someone and later date people who I thought loved me more than I loved them so if and when it ended, I thought I wouldn't feel as much pain. Wrong. Those endings have wreaked the most havoc and caused the most pain in my life. I chose to do what I thought others wanted me to do in my career so that they would be happy with me and I'd avoid the pain of disappointing them, keep the peace and make money. Wrong. Doing that caused me to feel creatively dead. I lost my money and they were mad at me anyway. I avoided confronting family and friends about words they have said and hurt they have inflicted with those words and deeds in the hope of preserving the relationship. Wrong. There is no relationship to preserve in instances in which I have expressed my truth to others about things they have said and in return they failed to acknowledge my pain and change their behavior.

Such a response invalidates my feelings. I've learned the most about myself and about my life through difficult and painful situations. The most important lesson I've learned is that I can feel the pain and survive it and because I've felt it and walked through it, I can now thrive. I will no longer be wasting my energy trying to avoid pain, but I'll be re-directing that energy to living and enjoying a fruit-bearing life. Don't be a victim living in your pain. Feel it, understand it, then move on and live.

The point of this book is to say something brash and bold and daring like: Big Fat Negro, Get Your Lazy Ass Off Of My Couch. Now had I expressed my real feelings years ago instead of burying them the title of this book would be: I'm slightly offended by your actions and you've hurt my feelings and I really need for you to hear me right now so that down the road this doesn't become a huge stumbling block in our relationship. But I never spoke up, which has created problems in my life. Maybe I never spoke up because I can better express myself through the written word. Here I can be ballsy. Here I can say: it really pisses me off and hurts my feelings that you (insert offense here) so don't do it again, motherfella. I've learned to speak up in life because when some form of self-flagellation occurs later. The not speaking up part has to do with fear and fear is what got me in the marital ditch and economic ditch of my life.

CHAPTER SIXTEEN
So Long Farewell and Adieu To Fear

So here are some of my great fears. Maybe they are some of yours too.

FEAR: I don't want to seem too needy.

TRUTH: We're all needy. Why do you think God created Eve? Because Adam was lonely. Do not be afraid of needing anyone. Our Lady Of Wondrous Singing a.k.a. Barbra Streisand should sing her song "People" as our world anthem.

FEAR: Even if I ask for what I really want, I won't get it. So why bother asking.

TRUTH: Well that's stupid because I already don't have it, which is why I have to ask for it in the first place. Black people first asked our government to enforce the constitution and give us our inalienable rights like the right to go to college and to vote and to be seated at lunch counters or on a bus, but were turned away and rather impolitely with fire hoses and bats and cowardly men clad in white sheets who enjoyed throwing bricks through windows and had a penchant for arson, especially of Christian symbols. Now if those who came before me had not even asked the question, who knows where we'd all be? What I do know is that the worst thing that could happen to me if I ask for something is that I'll be met with a fire hose or a blunt instrument to my head and that is not going to happen. So really the worst thing that could happen is the answer is no and that doesn't change my situation, but it does reduce the acid in my stomach from building up because I was too chicken shit to ask the question. Which really underscores the famous quote: *there is nothing to fear except fear itself.* Because fear is a cruel mistress, like one of the ones from the *Fifty Shades of Grey* but without a safe word and it keeps beating you down until you can't get back up again.

FEAR: I can't confront people on their bullshit because they may not like me or become angry with me.

TRUTH: Well here's the thing, if someone is lying to you, or leading you on, or being deceitful or mean-spirited, or perhaps telling you she can't come to your party because she can't get a babysitter, but then she posts pictures on Facebook of the cooler party she attended instead of yours (that never happened to me three or four times), she's really not worth your time. Or perhaps someone is clearly prejudiced against you or inhumane or unfair. Well guess what? You have no reason to like him so why would you care if he likes you back or he's angry with you for confronting him? If he is treating you so poorly, clearly he did not like or respect you so checking him on his misbehavior doesn't change your situation because it's already a pretty shitty one.

Telling these types of people off is really an act of kindness upon him and society as a whole. By telling him about his bad behavior you're doing him a service because clearly his parents checked out somewhere along the way which is why he turned out to be such a despicable person with horrific manners and or prejudices. There are so many people who I wish I had told off, or told them about themselves. Of course, I wish I did it eloquently, succinctly, with a touch of sarcasm and no evidence of my own pit stains, but that has rarely happened. Recently I wish I told someone off, but I was working for him so I had fear he'd take away my money, which he kind of couldn't do because I had a contract, but I've had contracts before and they didn't work out so well in my favor. Anyway, this asshole, I mean person with whom I've forgiven, fired me anyway, and I never gave him an eloquent, succinct piece of my mind. I'd like to give someone the really good piece of my mind in the form of a verbal assault that is so erudite they don't even get some of it until later when they go to Dictionary.com and look up some of the SAT words I used as weapons of mass personal annihilation. I do long to be more confrontational in my life and less afraid of the controversy because people who aren't a part of the fight are just spectators. Not that I want to fight. I want peace, but peace requires me to speak up. I don't want to sit on the sidelines of my life. I don't want to just talk about what I wish I did or what someone else had the guts to do in the ring. My goal is to stop complaining to others and my therapist (mostly my therapist because I'm on a budget) about someone else's misdeeds, but to actually call that motherfella or mothersister out on his or her bullshit and say I'm not shoveling that up anymore, but in a loving, forgiving way. So either clean up your act or move it along. Actually in my brief time as a confrontationist, I've learned that when you tell people they are full of shit, or they need to get their shit together, or you just call them on their shit, or simply tell the truth and expose their shit, they may go off on you at first, but later after they've recovered from the direct confrontation, they understand they can't get over on you anymore. They have more respect for you and they won't pull anymore bullshit with you because you've shown and told them you're sick of their shit and won't take it anymore. (Really shit was the best word to use to illuminate my point here.)

Although social media has now turned life into the cool kid's lunch table and it's all about popularity, looking cool, happy and rich on Instagram and people liking you on Facebook, or retweeting your tweet, or following you on Pinterest, Twitter or liking your pins, or your blog posts or your morning bowel movement, who really cares if someone likes you or not? Most of the people who are trying to get popular on social media are doing it to make money, not because they have this inner need for everyone "to really, really like them" to quote Sally Field. And Sally, I loved you in *Norma Rae* and *Places of The Heart* and any movie where you were being mistreated, but rose above your circumstances with grit and grace and often an Academy Award.

My Sally digression aside, really it's about not just liking yourself, because there are days that I like my hair and my outfit and my sense of humor, but it's about loving yourself on the days when you say something off color or idiotic, and your hairstylist accidentally put the wrong color on your hair, which makes it fall out so you have to wear a hat for three months (that only happened to me once). It's about loving yourself, bear-hugging your flaws and trusting your spirit to guide you through life and not external forces e.g.: Facebook to tell you how you should feel about yourself based on likes or visits to your blog. Your voice is the one that matters most (unless it's telling you to harm yourself or others) listen to your voice and trust it. Don't even listen to your mother. There I said it. I can say it because I am a mother so it's like intra-racism, which is the tolerable kind. That's a joke. No racism is tolerable.

I was set free of the fear that I was somehow not measuring

up in life when I understood that I am not what anybody says about me. I am not my bank account, or my résumé, or my list of screen credits. When I got that in my heart and my bones, I was set free. I understood it cognitively, intellectually, but I would still look at my popularity meter on IMDB (internet movie database) and when I couldn't tell someone what exciting project I was working on, I felt like I was walking in a diminished capacity. When I felt my worth in my heart and my soul is when I was liberated from the worldly definition of value and was able to walk in my inherent value as a spiritual, human soul created by God.

Fear causes you to settle for mediocrity then negatively weighs in and says you don't deserve greatness. Ignore both voices. But it may not be enough to ignore them because chances are those voices have been playing on a loop in your head for decades so you must replace them with uplifting words of belief, faith and perseverance.

Understand that the first person in your life that instilled fear is where it all began. We live in a fearful world so those thoughts get to us early. If you have fear, it's something you've been learning and perfecting for years. If it began at age two and now you're forty-two, then you've been a student at Fear University for forty years and have received every degree possible in the subject. So now you've got to unlearn forty years worth of crap. I replace it with scripture, which even if you don't believe in God or that the Bible contains the words of God or even God-inspired words, the truth is there are nice, uplifting words in the bible. 2 Timothy 1:7 "For God did not give us a spirit of fear, but a spirit of power, of love and self-discipline."

If you conquer fear daily, and it has to be a daily practice, then you won't end up having to kick the big, fat, loser off your couch whether it be at home, the office or anywhere else. You won't allow them to take up space in your life because fear is what gets them on the couch and negativity is what keeps them there.

In some ways we get trapped onto the treadmills of our lives where exhaustion and dissatisfaction become the norm so joy, hope, rest and peace are like foreign countries. While on the treadmill of life one doesn't stop to wade in a present moment of small beauty because we're always moving to the next task. We don't stop to assess our own thoughts or feelings so we employ others' desires and thoughts into our tasks because we're not fully awake. We're just passing through our own lives on this treadmill. My treadmill slowed down for a bit during my divorce, but picked back up so I continued to move through my life without feeling it, then during my economic collapse my treadmill broke down and I didn't have the money to repair it, but what I did have was time. Time without distractions because there was no work, so no one was calling me about work. My son was at an age where he didn't need my hovering. He was also spending most of the time with his father. Instead of putting a band-aid on leaky faucets of my life I had the time and the desire to get to the source of the leak. I finally had the courage to un-stiffen my upper-lip and ask for help. There weren't any distractions, so I could hear my intuition and listen to the Holy Spirit guide me. I could finally stop and give myself the time and space to actually feel my life and not just watch it pass me by on the treadmill. This valley has given me the gifts. I once had a life that was ruled by fear, which has now been replaced with faith, compassion, humility, trust in the spirit, discernment, wisdom, forgiveness, understanding, overflowing love and gratitude. I don't sit in judgment of my past, but look with wonder into my future and give thanks for the journey that continues.

Today I am content. Yes, I would like for some things to change and I'd like to grow in some areas and shrink in others (My upper thighs specifically). I am no longer seeking new circumstances to make me happy. I'm happy on my own. I'm grateful in every moment. Don Miguel Ruiz wrote that: "Happiness can only come from inside of us." And inside is where I look for happiness everyday.

CHAPTER SEVENTEEN

Almost Divorced

The period from the date I filed for divorce to the actual date my divorce was final was approximately two years. I spent two years in marital purgatory. There wasn't a box to check off for that when filling out applications or information sheets of any kind. I was in no man's land. Having to tell a prospective suitor you're almost divorced is as attractive as saying you're a little pregnant. My time in purgatory allowed for a lot of reflection and tremendous growth, but before the reflection and the growth, I chose to fight. I even went to court during my divorce. I engaged lawyers and paid them a tremendous amount of money. About three months into that two-year period, I stopped fighting and that is when I started learning, growing and making room to love again, because the thing about fighting and war is there is no room for love.

Divorce Wars

Back in 2001, George W. Bush and his cohorts started fabricating information about weapons of mass destruction. They got the American public all riled up about fighting the war on terror in Iraq. They developed a Crayola-like color bar pattern of warnings, created hype and then finally we went to war and were told this was a war we could win, but what have we won? It's been over a decade and I'm still not sure what was won.

That is divorce; a war that cannot be won. Divorce is a war that one chooses to manufacture, but understand that choice is just setting you up to lose. If friends, lawyers, others tell you to go fight, you can fight, but there is no finish line with a big trophy and roses at the end of your divorce. Others may recommend a fight, but what are they basing that recommendation on and what do they have at stake? When you engage in war there is always carnage, death, and destruction, so understand that if you decide to go to war against your spouse, that's what you'll get.

One of my favorite movies is *Cold Mountain*, which depicted the carnage and destruction during the Civil War. If the definition of winning a war is killing more of their guys than our guys, then the definition of winning a divorce war is metaphorically killing your soon to be ex-spouse and the casualties of this event are: children, savings, retirement, 401k, house, college funds, self-esteem, health, friends and family. Is all that carnage necessary? Isn't it enough to say to the world, "I don't want this person anymore," which is essentially what you're saying in the dissolution of a marriage? When you file for divorce you're basically telling the court, public records and the world that you're returning your husband. You're essentially saying, "I'm completely dissatisfied with my purchase of this spouse and I'm giving him back forever. It has a manufacturer's defect and I'm returning it within the warranty expiration period." Or if you're a child or acting like a child you're saying, "No backs to infinity and beyond." Divorce can be an ugly, long, depleting and debilitating civil war. You are seceding from a union.

I have friends who lovingly and jokingly re-named the movie *Cold Mountain* to *Cold Sore Mountain* and that's what divorce can be like if you continue to fight, it's like a cold sore that keeps coming back. You think it's gone, but then stress increases and it shows up on your lip again all blistery, festering and gross. Cold sores are caused by the herpes virus, which has no cure. It can be dormant or wide-awake and inflamed. Cold sore battles are analogous to divorce battles. There's no winning. It's always there and stress just exacerbates it. My advice for cold sores and divorce is to find a way to call a truce and make peace with the situation because fighting just prolongs a war that can't be won.

Nobody wins in divorce, but there are three bonuses. You rid yourself of the scourge that is your mother-in-law. Or better yet forgive her and yourself. You don't spend anymore time thinking about your marital problems. The arguing ceases.

Divorce Manners

People behave badly in a divorce. There was a time in the '90's when folks were getting fired and going postal because their identity, title, and money were being taken away from them in one fell swoop. It's very similar when a spouse drops the axe of divorce. In an instant your life changes. You are no longer a husband or wife; therefore, your title is taken away. You are being asked to leave the marriage; your house and your income will change dramatically. So people go postal when you ask for a divorce. That doesn't mean it's okay to behave badly, but it does explain the bad behavior. I do have empathy for jilted spouses because beneath that angry veneer is terror, pain, sadness, abandonment and a whole host of other scary emotions. But beyond divorce there is hope, peace and love. There is even the possibility to regain respect for your ex and compliment him or her in their parenting skills. You may even find yourself praying for your ex and I don't mean praying for their demise, but praying for their best. Life can surprise you in unimaginable ways that turn out better than anything you could have written. Breaking up and getting divorced always seem like an end, but if you are open, these endings in our lives can be the beginning of everything.

Anger is okay and a necessary stage of grief. Hey, if I hadn't been angry I would have never come up with the title of this book. Just don't get stuck in anger. The anger will overwhelm every aspect of your life. It will bleed into every relationship, every human and non-human interaction. It will eat you alive until you stop feeling, stop-seeing life unfold before you, stop taking deep breaths--essentially, until you're dead. You'll turn into this resentful, angry, shallow breathing, zombie trudging through an existence. Not a life. You may have fleeting moments that are a temporary respite from your anger, but when you laugh it will be so conspicuous that the moment of levity will be curtailed by your realization that you have to get your anger back. You'll become so accustomed to it that anger will be your identity.

Is that who you want to be? An angry pain-body, schlepping through life leaving your angry droppings as proof that you marked your territory? Anger doesn't benefit or expand your life. It doesn't make you blossom, shine, or make your life exude love, light and welcoming warmth.

The other side of anger is joy and after going through the muck of a break-up or divorce you deserve the joy. There is also gratitude, which is the first step towards joy. I am so thankful for what I walked through. I think I got my Master's degree in me while reflecting, crying and talking through my divorce and break-ups. I'm grateful I was married. I'm grateful I was blessed with a child and I'm grateful that he has a wonderful father. I'm grateful that we're better parents and people, having gotten past our grief and anger over the dissolution of our union. Our marriage may not have been the best, but there was a greater purpose to our coming together than I may ever know. Certainly our child we created together was predestined and not by us. Think about how hard it is to meet a guy, maintain a relationship and plan a wedding. There were so many times that I could have gotten off of that path to marriage. There were so many times that I could have not accepted dates from guys. If we don't put ourselves out there as vulnerable babes in the dating woods, we will never get to where we're supposed to be. I don't believe in mistakes and I look at everything in my life as a lesson. So in my life lessons of enduring relationships--good, bad, mediocre, easy, tortuous, abusive, happy, brief, painful, loving--I've learned, whether the lessons bring you down and build you up, they all have value. This is the knowledge I pass onto you with love and gratitude.

I'm not an angry, bitter woman. I am a woman who has been through something and went through anger, grief and many other stages to get to the other side. I am a woman who feels compassion for her female friends as we face the harrowing task of meeting a mate and all that it encompasses. I am a woman who has heard the same stories too many times and given my friends the same advice so often that I started to say I'm going to write a book and because I am also a woman of purpose, I wrote the damn thing. I love men and I love women and I wish that we really could get along better, but we're all broken people and we're trying to heal through relationships with others when sometimes we need to heal on our own before we come together with someone else. But then sometimes we need to heal with others. God didn't put us here alone so we've got to figure out how to do life better together and my hope is that this book will make you laugh, think and try to expect more from yourself and others.

Divorce and the Price Is Right

Remember when Katie Holmes came out and shocked the world and Tom Cruise with her stealth ninja assassin-like divorce that was filed and closed within a week? That will never happen to you. You are not a celebrity. Regular people's divorces take years and all of their resources because the lawyers find some kind of way to get paid even if you and your spouse end up broke. If you're incredibly efficient and totally agreeable it may only take months to file the paperwork and get your divorce decree from the court, but that is the exception.

Perhaps you're familiar with the song: "I fought the Law." The lyrics in that song conclude that the law won. Well, the law and lawyers are the only winners in divorce. So don't fight because the song has already told you, you're going to lose. The law wins. The law takes you down, drowns you in paperwork and will take all of your money if you keep fighting. If your attorney tells you that you will have your day in court, he or she is looking at you as the down payment for their new car, house or their kid's college tuition. You may emerge from your divorce unable to pay for your kid to go to college, but the lawyer's son is going to Princeton on YOU.

There is some mythical belief that you will have your day in court and if you can just explain to the judge why your spouse was such a jerk and checked out of the marriage, you won't have to pay; they will validate you and commend you and tell you you're right. WRONG, dummy (I say that with love). The judge punches numbers into a computer and the computer spits out the answer and that's your day in court. You actually don't need a judge or lawyer for any of it because the computer does it all. You just need a person who knows how to work that computer program. And guess what? I know people who have been able to figure it out on their own. It's kind of like doing your own taxes. The computer program for divorce and child custody in California is called a Dissomaster. It's called a master because it's in charge and makes decisions about your life, but computers are in charge of everything anyway, right? Dissomaster: friend or foe. Think of the Dissomaster as the Stairmaster. You may hate it, but it gets results. While on the Stairmaster there is pain, but the end result is a tight ass. The end result of the Dissomaster is you don't have to call the fat ass on the couch your husband or wife anymore. I guess that's more of a consolation prize than anything else.

I stated before that the only real winners who emerge from a divorce are the attorneys and the prize they claim is based on what you spend on them. They can get: a new car, a house, or a remodeled kitchen. For attorneys divorces are like *The Price Is Right.* You enter their office and they start guessing what your price is and the closer they get to the price the closer they get to the showcase showdown. If you're a big fool, with bigger pockets and a sense of entitlement and need to have your day in court, your attorney may win both showcases that include trips around the world, a brand new RV, a new car and barbecue grill. Please don't waste your money on a divorce attorney. Your money is better spent on a therapist, at least there you will get validation and maybe even guidance.

When some of you enter a divorce attorney's office, he views you as a winning lottery ticket. Be practical, forgive, move on and save your money. Why are people so indignant to think they will win in court when in this country we have to have an organization like The Innocence Project because there are wrongly accused prison inmates who have been imprisoned for decades and/or on death row awaiting execution? They had their day in court, were innocent and convicted anyway. Courts are obviously not always about justice so why bother when there is no justice or fairness in a divorce? The world isn't fair. If you didn't learn that in kindergarten, that will be an expensive lesson to learn in divorce. Fairness, just like beauty, is in the eye of the beholder. Save your money for your children, your retirement or just buy your own showcase prizes and hire Drew Carey to make an appearance and deliver your stuff. He's probably cheaper and more fun than any divorce lawyer.

Don't be afraid of the courtroom, the judge, his lawyer or your ex-husband in the setting of the courtroom. This is the same man who couldn't pick up his socks, hold his liquor, or balance a checkbook. The only difference now is he's got a well dressed overly paid lawyer by his side. You all are the same people just in a different location. Don't be scared of the circumstance. Your tax dollars helped pay for this courthouse so basically this is your house. Enter with that attitude. Do not be intimidated.

Keep in mind that if your spouse lost his or her manners during the marriage, I guarantee you he will be impolite during the divorce. Impolite is a nice way of saying he will be a first class asshole. I had a friend who was getting divorced and her mother passed away during her divorce proceedings. The day her mother passed away, her soon to be ex-husband called (knowing her mother had died) and asked her for reimbursement for a bill he paid for their child. No manners, no compassion, or as my mother would say, "Uncouth."

Money Won't Make It Hurt Less

Hurting your spouse where he lives in his wallet is not going to make the pain of being dumped go away. It's not even going to ease it. Alimony is blood money in a way. Something had to die for you to get that cheddar. It's necessary for some to receive alimony, but others take advantage. Don't drag out your divorce as a means to make your spouse spend more money on lawyers and the process and think that's going to eradicate your anger and hurt. Whether the husband pays or the wife pays, both of you will pay financially, emotionally and physically. Your children will pay as well.

Marriages and relationships don't die suddenly like death by a car crash. They are usually prolonged cancer-like deaths. At first, you ignore or excuse the symptoms until they become no longer ignorable. You manage until you've had enough. But be awake to the reality and don't simply blame your spouse for the demise of the relationship. Look inward. Take responsibility. Learn, grow, and change. Become a better human being in the midst of the pain.

The Grass May Be Greener

Marriage is forever. Let's think about that. I mean, seriously contemplate forever or at least until death. How many things in your life do you think you're going to hold onto forever? Let's face it, some of our once most treasured items will end up being haggled over in a yard sale and will probably go for pennies. The only material item I'm keeping around forever is my size 28 Levis that I intend to fit back into someday. I've had them for seventeen years. They have taken up residence in the back of my closet, but will get moved up when my hip measurements move down. Seventeen years is the longest committed relationship I've ever been in with something that has actually lived with me and moved to new residences with me. The thing about those jeans is they don't talk, or yell, or fail to do something I've asked them to do, or flirt with other women, so it's an easy relationship. The jeans do spite me, but they are so far back in the closet that I can't see them do that every day.

When you sign up for marriage, that's forever. Your husband will be there every single day and he's not as neutral, quiet, or unassuming as the jeans. He's in your face, pushing your buttons and neglecting to recognize all your efforts to keep a tidy, happy home, cute figure and maintain your roots all at the same time. A marital relationship is not like the one you have with your hairstylist: two bad haircuts and then it's over. You wouldn't endure two years of horrific hair fiascos, only clinging to the hope of what you used to have and what can be again. You'd fire your stylist, but it's not that easy to fire your husband. Don't be in such a hurry to get married. You know what goes well with engagement chicken: honesty and a prenup. Marriage is a read the fine print kind of decision. It's not the quickly click agree button decision you make because you want to wear the white dress and toss the bouquet so you can say, "I'm married, bitches, but you're still single."

Marriage is selfless, compassionate business. The first part of this book was about honoring self, standing up for yourself, and believing you deserve the best. All of those points are still valid, especially in marriage. It is only after you've learned to value yourself that you can value a mate. Don't leave your marriage or relationship because you want greener grass. Someone's grass will always be greener. Tend to your own garden.

Here's the thing about greener grass, you don't know what other people are putting on their grass to make it look that way. It could be some harmful chemical that brings out the green hue and appear to be lush and thriving, but really that's a ruse and underneath it's just a withering, dry mess. The woman sitting next to you may have perkier boobs, but do her boobs bear the battle scars from nursing a baby, or a husband or boyfriend who is a boob man? Maybe God didn't even give her those boobs, but Dr. Beverly Hills Plastic Surgeon did. In which case down the road she may have a boob leakage, or explosion and have to get them replaced. Don't look at your neighbor's grass or boobs. Value what you have.

Adopt the Surfer Attitude In Your Divorce

If you're facing a divorce or are in the midst of it, you must remember that the bottom line is: this is not going to kill you. When I was getting divorced my ex-husband's lawyer inundated me with so much paperwork that it felt like I had a second job. I had to hire a babysitter to watch my kid while I completed this paperwork. Recently a girlfriend was going through a divorce and she too was deluged by paperwork. It was overwhelming to her. Also seeing it all in print -- his declaration about her behavior in the marriage, his condemnation of her as a wife and a mother--played mind tricks on her. It nearly broke her spirit and incited anger. I told her what I'm going to tell you. This is not a life-threatening illness that could literally remove you from this earth. It's paperwork. It's a nuisance, but you have to do it. It doesn't mean anything really. The paperwork is just a means by which the lawyers can charge more money. Yes, the judge will read over your declarations, but don't treat this paperwork like it's the Constitution. It's just words on a page. This all is just a process that feels painful, but it too will end. It is a death, but you can continue living after your marriage dies and you can live even more fully. You can thrive. If you've been in a bad marriage you've been oppressed. Soon you will be able to say: "Free at last, free at last, thank God almighty I'm free at last." Make sure you live once you get your freedom.

I was able to tell my friend somewhat blithely, "It's just paperwork" in part because I went through a divorce and learned first hand that declarations don't make or break a divorce, but also because I have surfed. Several years ago, I had the privilege to vacation in Maui and learn how to surf. I got to know the surfing instructors at the place where I took lessons and started hanging out with them socially. These were people who spent their days floating on waves and living in paradise. They were the antithesis of my neurotic energy, but by the end of my vacation, I had appropriated the island mentality. I was no longer looking at my watch, annoyed that my vacation excursion was beginning late, or wondering if I'd have some time in the afternoon before dinner to get some work done while on vacation. The grandiosity of the ocean, the mere existence and beauty of this creation of God allowed me to see how small my problems and divorce paperwork were in the larger scheme of life. I began to walk with ease and calm. I suppose this is the mentality we are supposed to take on while on vacation and the hope is that we'll bring some of it back to the mainland and incorporate it into our lives, but that hardly ever happens because mainland life becomes too hectic and we forget our island mentality. Part of the island mentality and vacation thinking is that because we are unencumbered by the busyness of our lives, our thoughts can remain in the present moment.

The mentality needed when facing a divorce or break-up is this moment-to-moment, mindful, present tense thinking. One can only handle the task or decision and moment in front of her. It's too overwhelming in a loss (which is what a divorce is) to think about moments that aren't here yet. Tomorrow is not guaranteed anyway, so think about how much energy it takes to worry about tomorrow and use that energy to deal with what's in front of you today. The surfers knew that their tomorrow would be spent floating, paddling and moving with the waves of the ocean so that probably made their laid-back attitude easier to accomplish. Also, I think some of them smoked weed, which contributed to their general ease. I'm not advocating drug use, but use your mind, your thoughts and your attitude to cultivate a peaceful, present energy field to get through each moment. If all else fails just take a moment, breathe and imagine you're a surfer, floating, riding a wave and bring that island thinking onto the mainland.

The ocean waves mimic our lives. Things come in and they go back out like the waves, and it continues rhythmically, methodically over and over again. This loss of your marriage doesn't mean life won't continue. The divorce is a wave, a big wave that may toss you around, but another wave is coming to lift you up and another one after that will come and perhaps you'll be able to ride it fearlessly with ease and joy and peace that only the ocean can bring. Your divorce is not the end of the world, it's just a rough wave. Don't give it more negative gravitas than it already has. It's a choppy wave that you won't be riding forever. There's another wave coming and who knows where that ride will take you.

Love and Compassion In Divorce Yes, It's Possible

We hold marriages to be sacred and acknowledge the spiritual aspect in readings at wedding about love. 1 John 4:11 reads: "Beloved, if God loved us, we also ought to love one another." This command to love one another doesn't have any caveats to it. It doesn't say love them, until we're tired of loving them. It doesn't say love them until they stop making enough money or agreeing with us. It just says we ought to love one another. Let's face it, sometimes it's hard to love people, especially when you're getting a divorce. I think we need to practice something radical in divorce and if we do, we'll experience a peace that transcends understanding. We need to love our exes and ourselves through a divorce.

If you say there is no love, you must love yourself enough to give love back to them through this difficult trial in life that you are both facing. Love keeps no record of wrongs; it is long suffering. Even if they don't love you back, you must extend love to them. The love you extend will have a powerful transformative effect on you both and on the entire process. If your ex-husband tries to do something to you that is unfair, or devious, and you meet that act with love there will be no discord because love forgives. Love will be your Teflon shield during the divorce so that everything that is meant to hurt, embitter, anger or destroy you will slide off of your Teflon love shield.

If the Teflon love shield analogy doesn't work for you or you're not anywhere near a place of love, my advice is to keep a sneeze guard lengths distance between you and your ex. So when your ex says some crazy shit to rile you up let it hit that imaginary sneeze guard first and not you. Many soon to be exes argue as a means to continue the connection. Just like children may act out to receive attention even if it's negative attention, your ex may be after the same thing: your attention.

They will engage you in arguing because it keeps you together longer, even if it's a negative connection because they aren't ready to cut the cord. The antidote is to agree. If your soon to be ex says the sky is yellow with pink polka dots--just agree with him or her and the argument dies.

Nelson Mandela spent twenty-seven years in prison, but upon his release he forgave his captors. He worked alongside his so-called enemies who oppressed, suppressed and imprisoned people in the name of racism. Mandela stood for peace. Peace is a form of love. If Nelson Mandela can use love, peace and forgiveness to end an oppressive, violent, racist government then I surely know that love can be practiced in divorce. Practice is key. I'm not saying it's going to come to you naturally. That's why you need your bridesmaids for support during your divorce. Carrying your bouquet and holding your wedding dress while you pee is a glamorous job compared to standing by someone as they go through a divorce. A divorce maid's duties include but are not limited to: holding the ex-bride's hair back when she pukes from imbibing to numb the pain and loneliness, preventing drunk dialing or texting, spying on the ex's new girlfriend and collecting dirt on them both, arranging hot hook-ups for the divorcée and planning the divorce party. Choose your divorce maids carefully. Strutting down the aisle and working on a hook-up with a groomsman is one thing, but standing beside someone down the tumultuous road of life and divorce is so much more. When I went through a divorce one of my dearest friends, Burnie, came to my apartment and told me that, "We are a family and we'll get through this together." Those heartfelt words were followed by action that buoyed my spirit, and enabled me to get through those post marriage years.

The end of my marriage was a loss and I had to go through the stages of grief and feel sadness, anger, and pain. However, I didn't get stuck in those feelings. The loss does not define me. The loss has now become a gain. I love my ex-husband. I no longer introduce myself as divorced. I no longer tell people within a few minutes of meeting them that I paid alimony. I don't wear that moniker like it's a red badge of courage. When we allow a loss to define us we victimize ourselves. When we allow a loss to become a gain we are no longer just survivors of the loss, but we thrive.

A Divorce Prayer

Lord help me to not run my ex-husband over with a car, cuss him out, clench my jaw until it locks over that motherfella's triflin' ways.

That's a prayer of desperation and anger. My prayers are for my ex-husband's best. We are forever linked as parents. You can find and practice love in a divorce. Romans 13:10 "Love does no wrong to one's neighbor (it never hurts anybody)." If we honor the commandment: "Love your neighbor as you do yourself," then we are certainly called to love our exes as we would our neighbors. Love doesn't hurt. It doesn't play dirty. It takes the higher road.

Dare to have compassion for this person with whom you shared a bed, a life and perhaps share a child or children. Finish things how you started. You entered this covenant with love, thanksgiving, compassion and kindness. It's possible to exit it the same way. I wish I had done it better. My hope is that someone else can and will do better. Die to your ego and open up your heart and spirit to your former mate who is hurting as much as you. Acknowledge the death of the relationship, but extend kindness, forgiveness and love to one another as you separate.

Here is what some may consider the most controversial sentence in this whole book: I love my ex-husband. It's extremely counterculture to feel that way let alone confess it. I know that sounds criminally insane to many of you. I'm sure there are some of you who just threw this book down in disgust, or angrily turned off your e-book reader. Well, turn it back on. I don't love him in the romantic sense. I don't ever want to be married to him again. Entangled in forgiveness and gratitude is love. So because I have forgiven and I am so grateful, I have love for my ex-husband. It's possible to love your ex again. It's possible you still do love your ex, but the circumstances have subdued the love and the miscommunication has distorted it, but the love never fails. The marriage failed.

I have love for all of my exes because they have taught me invaluable lessons in life and love. Those are roads I do not need to travel again because I know where they lead. They are bridges to heartache and nowhere. Yet I am thankful for the lessons and experience.

The Art of Divorce

Divorces like marriages and wine take time to get better. A good divorce has withstood a lot of tests, but communication has remained intact. You and your ex have grown apart together and are stronger for it. One day you and your ex can become a model divorced couple, the kind of divorced couple that others aspire to be: a divorced power couple. There is hope that you can be the kind of divorced couple that other people boast about. You could even be a divorced super couple like those super couples from '80's soap operas: Angie and Jesse from *All My Children*, Patch and Kayla from *Days Of Our Lives*, and the ultimate soap super couple: Luke and Laura from *General Hospital*. There is actually a chance that you and your ex will be a better-divorced couple than many married couples. You need clear, concise communication in a happy divorce. Highly functioning divorced couples require mutual respect, clear boundaries, flexibility, understanding, appreciation, compassion, humility, patience, forgiveness and love. Many couples choose a reading from Corinthians during their weddings. I believe this reading needs to be an anthem during and after your divorce. Write it on note cards and tape it to your bathroom mirror, your car, and your forehead.

1 Corinthians 13:4-7

Love is patient, love is kind. It does not envy, it does not boast, it is not proud. It is not rude, it is not self-seeking, it is not easily angered, it keeps no record of wrongs. Love does not delight in evil, but rejoices with truth. It always protects, always trusts, always hopes, always perseveres. Love never fails.

For Good

I truly believe the old adage that people come into our lives for a reason a season or a lifetime. My ex-husband came into mine for all three. We are partners in parenting, which is a partnership that holds immense gravitas. God chose for us to be together and in our brief union blessed us with a son. I know that marriage was a predestined path.

You may believe your ex partner, boyfriend or mate is a

crazy, good for nothing loser, but you made a choice to walk down an aisle, take an oath or in some other form distinguish this person as yours. There was something within you that attracted this mate. It could have been the brokenness that you both had in common. So please understand that I'm not pointing the finger at the big, fat, loser on the couch. I'm saying to look inward at why you allowed that person to take up residence in your life and on your couch. Know that if you have a loser somewhere on your metaphorical couch in life that you're sitting right there next to him or her; eating the chips, flipping the channels and perpetuating the zombie bliss. Recognize it's not just him. It's you. Perhaps there is something you needed to learn or go through with this person which is why he showed up in your life and you allowed him to sit on your couch, but when it's time to go or evict him from your couch, do not dawdle. Be on your way and thank him for the journey and lesson, then take your relationship education and graduate. Some of us are like college students a.k.a. super seniors who stay in school too long and are afraid to graduate. Most universities kick you out if you haven't matriculated in seven years. Please don't be that fool. Learn your lesson and move on.

If you have children with your ex or soon to be ex, understand that your growth will dictate the parameters of the continued parental partnership. Don't expect change from your parenting partner, but you will change how you interact with that person because you've elevated your standards. They won't meet you down where you used to be unless you stay there. They will be forced to rise up to you. Who knows? That may be part of their life lesson with you.

If you have children you need to answer to a higher calling, which means that you have to put your needs aside and your revenge, regret and sorrow and do what is best for the child. In the best interest of the child is a summons for all divorced parents. Don't be a crappy ex. Pay your alimony, or child support. Don't bad mouth your ex to your kids. Don't continue to fight in front of your kids. Be a decent human being so your children have an example to emulate. Respect and revere the gift that is your child. People have stopped regarding the birth of a child as the miracle that it is. Doctors don't even know why women go into labor after nine months. If something miraculous happens to you, then continue to treat that miracle with the awe and respect it deserves. Honor it by doing what's best for your child.

Give your ex-husband the space to be whatever kind of father he's going to be without judgment or criticism. He is the only biological dad your child will ever have. Unless he is endangering your child or children, allow him to parent to the best of his ability. Just because your ex was a big, fat, loser on your couch he still has value. His shit may be raggedy now, but don't hold that against him. At some point you co-signed onto that shit. Don't throw away your former spouse or boyfriend because they were terrible as husbands and mates. They can still be wonderful fathers.

They can also still be the jerks you were married to, but it's your duty to take the higher road of peace, patience and compassion. You'll have to have those difficult conversations with your ex, but it can be done with compassion, respect and with the helpful promptings of a therapist or social worker. You may have to learn how to threaten your ex in a non-threatening way if he's not acting right concerning the children you share. Here's the thing, you divorced this person for various reasons. They probably blamed the divorce on you. We're all culpable for our behavior, but if there was a specific issue in the marriage that your ex has not dealt with or is still in denial about, then that issue is going to resurface in his parenting. If he has an addiction, chances are he's not going to have time to parent because that addiction will supersede everything else. As the mother, even though you know your child's father has this problem it is up to you to rise above for the sake of your child and do all that is humanly possible to help your ex recognize his problem and get help, so that he can have a better relationship with his child otherwise his child will miss out on having a father and try to fill that void with an addiction of his or her own. Yes, that's hard because this is your child and you probably want to strangle the father for being such a big fat loser, but you have to breathe deeply. Listen to some Enya and pray for patience, compassion and a miracle for your child. If your ex has anger issues, be certain that these will manifest in parenting and your child may even mimic his or her father's temperament because that is what's been modeled. If your ex is codependent, your kid may be that way too. So guess what. Yes, it's your job to break the chain of the bad behavior for your child's sake. Get help. You may even have to go back to court and have the court mandate family therapy. It may get ugly, but remember growth is not pretty.

New Wives & Girlfriends Club

Remember when your ex husband was courting you and was all over you, showering you with attention, gifts, love etc. Well there will come a time when you're divorced or perhaps it occurred when you were married, hence the divorce, that he will discover New Pussy. New Pussy requires work, attention, money and time. When your ex is chasing after this new woman, he may neglect his children. You need to call him on it. Yes, it's a difficult conversation, but this is for the health and welfare of your child. His new woman may even have her hand in his pocket and have the audacity to question how much he pays or should pay in child support. And yes, your ex motherfella husband may even bring that nonsense up with you. Please do not hesitate to take him back to court or threaten court or call him out on his ridiculous thinking and raggedy ways. A man who puts the desires of new pussy above his children needs some sense knocked into his head. If you can't do that, then call his momma, sister, brother, best friend or someone else who can. If those people are triflin', have the tough conversation and look out for your child. And lastly pray for the father of your children to be the man and dad your child needs because he is the only person on this earth with that title and we all want the best for our kids.

Sidney Poitier said, "The measure of a man is how well he takes care of his children." You and your ex are in the trenches of parenthood together. My ex-husband is my parenting partner, which often vexes our son who cannot pit us against one another. He's even said it's annoying that his dad and I are on the same team. Our child is our priority.

If you do your divorce, or your pivotal break-up right, you'll be changed for the better. You'll move onto better and more fulfilling relationships, even possibly with your ex. The lyrics from the song "For Good" in the musical *Wicked* beautifully sung by Kristin Chenoweth and Idina Menzel illustrate my point. Look them up. Let that *Wicked* song be your divorce/break-up anthem. Truly forgive, move on and have gratitude for the experience.

CHAPTER EIGHTEEN

FIGHT ON!

Remember those awkward, teenage years when you were growing and changing and becoming an adult. Growth may look frightening or messy from the outside, but it eventually feels fantastic on the inside. It can feel fantastic inside, while still looking bleak from an outsider's perspective, but when you know you're walking in truth and with the Spirit, you're headed in the best direction no matter what the circumstances. As I went through divorce and depression, job loss and financial collapse my friends and family were scared and worried for me because from the outside things didn't look so good, but they couldn't see what I was gaining inside. Inside growth becomes apparent outside, but it's not immediate. People are happy for you and cheering you on when they can see you've achieved something tangible, like the big job, or the big house or the ridiculously ostentatious, gas guzzling car, but I wish we could have people cheering us on through the loss in life, or valleys, hard times, break-ups, and break-downs because that's when you really need a pep squad. That is also when amazing growth occurs and blessings.

Now I'm diametrically opposed to the antiquated notion of cheerleaders in barely there clothes, dancing provocatively during intermission, i.e. The Laker Girls, The Dallas Cowboy cheerleaders, but I approve of the metaphorical cheerleaders in life. I've been blessed to have my own cheer squad who has been there for me, when I'm down seventeen points in the fourth quarter and it looks bleak, but they manage to continue to believe. They are the ones who have told me not to throw in the towel, to keep fighting. My Dad sent me letters for two years that always ended with, "keep the faith," which is difficult in the darkest hours, but I have kept the faith. And faith is the evidence of things unseen. We may not be able to see it, but we can still believe it.

I'm a USC alumni and our cheer slogan is: Fight On! While in college my classmate, Lyle, used to end his sentences with: "Fight On," which was such a profound and uplifting statement, although at the time I thought it kind of corny. I say that with love. While I attended USC, I never went to a football game, which is sort of sacrilegious and they might take away my diploma for admitting that publicly, but the slogan of Fight On has stayed in my sub-conscious. Thanks, Lyle. So in the words of Tommy Trojan, Fight On through divorce, break-ups, illness, job endings, bankruptcy and every loss imaginable, because after a loss there is always a gain. Fight On through the mess of your life and you will get the message and the miracle. Fight On! And in order to Fight On, you have to get off of your couch.

THE END

ABOUT THE AUTHOR

Sonja Warfield is a comedy writer who began her career writing for the Emmy-Award winning sitcom *Will & Grace*. From there she went on to write for the ABC comedy *Jake in Progress* and the hit BET series *The Game*, where she was executive story editor. She serves as co-producer for the BET series, *Zoe Ever After*. Ms. Warfield has had development deals with Sony Pictures Television that led to her writing pilots for NBC and ABC. Additionally, she has written two pilots for HBO. Ms. Warfield also writes feature films and has written an adaption of a novel into a screenplay for Alcon Entertainment and 2S, a Hilary Swank production company. Currently, she serves as an adjunct professor at The University Of Southern California School of Cinematic Arts where she earned her B.A. in Cinema-Television Critical Studies.

Sonja is also a proud mom to Mr. Norman. They live in Southern California where they spend a lot of time outdoors and not on the couch.

I love to keep in touch with my readers.
Please follow me on Twitter: https://twitter.com/Sonjawar
Instagram: https://instagram.com/Sonjawar
Check out my website: www.Sonjawarfield.com
Like me on Facebook: https://facebook.com/SonjaWarfield

<<<<>>>>

Made in the USA
San Bernardino, CA
07 March 2016